AF726004

Safda Mahmood is a Senior Solicitor and Advocate with Coventry City Council and nationally recognised Professional Development provider. Safda has been an approved member of the SRA list of CPD providers, and has practiced and lectured in Family Law for over 25 years. He is on the Law Society Children Law Accredited Panel, specialising in Children and Adoption Law. As an author, he has written for various publications, such as Jordans' Family Law Journal, The Legal Executives Journal, Solicitors Journal and the Law Society and Local Government Bulletin. Safda is co-author of the title 'Child Care and Protection: Law and Practice: Sixth Edition, and previous edition.

Covid-19 and Family Law in England and Wales

The Essential Guide

Covid-19 and Family Law in England and Wales

The Essential Guide

Safda Mahmood
Solicitor, Author and Lecturer

Law Brief Publishing

© Safda Mahmood

All rights reserved. No part of this publication may be reproduced, stored in a retrieval system, or transmitted, in any form or by any means, electronic, mechanical, photocopying, recording or otherwise, without the prior permission of the publisher.

Excerpts from judgments and statutes are Crown copyright. Any Crown Copyright material is reproduced with the permission of the Controller of OPSI and the Queen's Printer for Scotland. Some quotations may be licensed under the terms of the Open Government Licence (http://www.nationalarchives.gov.uk/doc/open-government-licence/version/3).

Cover image © iStockphoto.com/ronstik

The information in this book was believed to be correct at the time of writing. All content is for information purposes only and is not intended as legal advice. No liability is accepted by either the publisher or author for any errors or omissions (whether negligent or not) that it may contain. Professional advice should always be obtained before applying any information to particular circumstances.

Published 2020 by Law Brief Publishing, an imprint of Law Brief Publishing Ltd
30 The Parks
Minehead
Somerset
TA24 8BT

www.lawbriefpublishing.com

Paperback: 978-1-913715-11-3

This book is dedicated, in particular, to my son,
Hammad, where through him, I have regained
the inspiration to want to cherish those things
that are all too often taken for granted.

PREFACE

I am sure that you will agree that when we all approached 2020, and as is often done, New Year's resolutions and predictions were made, none of us would have thought that 2020 would turn out the way it currently has. The impact of Covid-19 has been felt across the world, and has touched us all in one way or another, whether in terms of health, psychologically, economically or socially.

At the time of writing, although in England and Wales, we have had approximately 12 weeks of 'lockdown', and as of 10 June 2020, and there has been some gradual easing of the social distancing restrictions, there is still a high level of anxiety, uncertainty, and many unknowns as to how the second half of 2020 will turn out, and in fact, the longer term thereafter.

As a family practitioner, I have seen the impact that Covid-19 has had across all areas of family law, and will continue to do so. This book will set out a practitioner's account of the significant impact of Covid-19, as far as family work is concerned. It will address specifically the way in which practices have changed, and have had to adapt as a result of social distancing.

There will be considerations of the following matters in particular:

- PRIVATE CHILDREN LAW CASES AND IMPACT OF COVID-19
- PUBLIC FUNDING IN FAMILY CASES, DIGITILISATION AND THE IMPACT OF COVID-19
- DOMESTIC ABUSE, SOCIAL DISTANCING AND COVID-19
- REMOTE HEARINGS, FAMILY LAW AND COVID-19

- PUBLIC CHILDREN AND ADOPTION LAW CASES AND IMPACT OF COVID-19

- DEPARTMENT OF EDUCATION GUIDANCE FOR CHILDREN'S SOCIAL CARE DEPARTMENTS IN ENGLAND

- WELSH GOVERNMENT GUIDANCE FOR CHILDREN'S SOCIAL CARE DEPARTMENTS IN WALES

Each of these matters will be discussed in turn, and the position in both England and Wales will be considered.

The law described in this book is believed to be correct and up-to-date on 10 June 2020.

Safda Mahmood
June 2020

CONTENTS

CHAPTER ONE
PRIVATE CHILDREN LAW CASES AND IMPACT OF COVID-19

INTRODUCTION

Many of you who are family law practitioners, will know that enforcement of child arrangements has got to be the most difficult areas of family law to be able to deal with, as there are often very strong emotions that are bedded in. This makes it very difficult for clients to be able to make compromises for the benefit of the child. Sometimes, clients will find it very difficult to be able to get past the hurt, upset, anxiety, anger, and sometimes bitterness, so as to see what is the child's best interests when it comes to agreeing and complying with child arrangements. Matters relating to enforcement and the impact of Covid-19 will be considered in this chapter.

WHAT ARE THE OPTIONS FOR ENSURING COMPLIANCE WITH ORDERS?

We have all had situations whereby we have had to consider what options are available to ensure that 'contact' takes place, as per the court order. As a reminder, many of you will be aware of the various options available, such as the following:

- Activity directions
- Activity conditions
- Enforcement orders
- Financial compensation

- Children being joined as parties through the r. 16.4 Family Procedure Rules 2010 (FPR 2010) procedure
- Directions being made under s.37 Children Act 1989 (CA 1989)
- Switching of Child Arrangements
- Costs orders
- Committal to prison for breach of an order and/or undertaking

These options above have their own difficulties. When it comes to seeking a costs order for example, although Part 28 FPR 2010 provides, at rule 28.1, for the court to make, at any time, such order as to costs as it thinks just, the reality is that if a court was to make a costs order, against the 'resident' parent for not abiding by requiring them to make the child available to spend time with the other parent, the costs order could inflame matters, and exacerbate the situation. Similarly, although there have been cases where the court have switched child arrangements, as recently as in the case of ***Re H (Parental Alienation) [2019] EWHC 2723 (Fam)***, there are always risks associated with switching residence. The court would need to carefully balance the associated risks in deciding whether to go with this option. In this case for example, this was the 6th set of private law proceedings between the parents in relation to the child, aged twelve. The child had been having regular contact with his father and his paternal family, which had been of good quality. Subsequently, the direct contact stopped. At paragraph 13, Keehan J, who heard the case, emphasised that the expert evidence was such that the child may, on the surface, appear to be fine emotionally, but he was not. If the court were to contemplate transferring residence from the mother to the father, there were risks to the child; he may run away and he may not settle in his father's care if it was not properly supported. In terms of the risks associated with 'parental alienation' the instructed expert opined that the mother was firmly entrenched in her view, and was most unlikely to change. It was advised that parental alienation was very harmful to a child. It skewed the child's ability to form any and all sorts of relationships, and was not limited to the failed relationship with the other parent. In this case, the expert stated that there was now, no other option, but to transfer residence to his father in the welfare best interests of this child. If, short of a transfer, an attempt was made to re-establish contact, the child, whilst remaining in his mother's care, was likely to become even more entrenched against his father.

HOW DO YOU ENSURE COMPLIANCE OF COURT ORDERS GIVEN SOCIAL DISTANCING RESTRICTIONS ARE IN PLACE?

During the middle of March 2020, when 'lockdown' was announced in England and Wales, immediately thereafter, there became apparent difficulties surrounding the practical aspects of reconciling imposed social distancing restrictions, and how parents were expected to abide by existing orders for child arrangements. Some obvious issues that arose were:

- What was to happen for example, if there was in place, a shared child arrangements order, which specified living with? (what used to be called a 'shared residence order', until the amendments bought in by the Children and Families Act 2014, on 22nd of April 2014)

- If the children were spending one week with mother, and the other week with their father, in different households, which household (if any), was to take priority?

- What if a child was currently residing in household A? Were they to stay there, by default, or was it dependent upon where they sought to reside?

- What about if one parent had the benefit of the child arrangements order, specifying spending time with? (What used to be called a contact order, until the amendments bought in by the Children and Families Act 2014, on 22nd of April 2014). Was that order still to be honoured?

- If the child was residing with mother for example, and the child arrangements order required for mother to make the child available to spend time with father, each and every Tuesday and Thursday, between the hours of 4 - 6pm, was this to happen?

These, and other questions became some much more prominent and real issues as a result of the social distancing restrictions. Taking the last of the above examples, relating to the contact which is to happen every Tuesday and Thursday, one could imagine that the mother may rely upon Covid-19, to justify the child *must not* be going to see and spend time with father because of the social distancing restrictions? Mother may be justified and excused for her genuine anxieties and worries if she was to allow here child to go in such circumstances, but what if she was to use the pandemic as a strategic ploy, to 'block' the contact with the father, with no or very little regard to the child's needs of maintaining a relationship with the father? We can all imagine that this is a real possibility in some, and it is hoped, a limited number of cases.

These and other questions led to a lot of anxiety and uncertainty amongst parents across the UK, and it was on 24 March 2020, that Sir Andrew McFarlane, President of the Family Division and Head of Family Justice, handed own some very vital, and essential guidance in this regard. This is considered further below.

CORONAVIRUS CRISIS: GUIDANCE ON COMPLIANCE WITH FAMILY COURT CHILD ARRANGEMENT ORDERS

This was handed down by Sir Andrew McFarlane (President of the Family Division and Head of Family Justice) on the 24 March 2020 The full guidance is available at the following link: **https://www.judiciary.uk/announcements/coronavirus-crisis-guidance-on-compliance-with-family-court-child-arrangement-orders/**

In this guidance, the President set out that during the current Coronavirus Crisis, some parents whose children are the subject of Child Arrangements Orders made by the Family Court, have been concerned about their ability to meet the requirements of these court orders safely in the wholly unforeseen circumstances that now apply. Therefore, this guidance is offered, although the circumstances of each child and family will differ, any therefore any advice can only be in the most general form.

PR Rests With the Parents

The President has set out that parental responsibility for a child who is the subject of a Child Arrangements Order (CAO) made by the Family Court, rests with the child's parents, and not with the court. It is emphasised that there is an expectation that parents will care for children by acting sensibly and safely when making decisions regarding the arrangements for their child and deciding where and with whom their child spends time.

Parents Must Abide by the Government Staying at Home Rules

The President set out that parents must abide by the 'Rules on Staying at Home and Away from Others' issued by the UK government on 23 March ['the Stay at Home Rules']. In addition to these Rules, advice about staying safe and reducing the spread of infection has been issued and updated by Public Health England and Public Health Wales ['PHE/PHW'].

At this point, before I go further into the guidance by the President, the reader should note that this guidance was issued in March 2020, at a point where the Stay at Home rules were set then. You do need to bear in mind that the Stay at Home Rules have since been updated, principally on the 13 May 2020, and more recently, on the 1 June 2020, with more changes due on the 15 June 2020. At the time of writing, on the 10 June 2020, we have in force, the Health Protection (Coronavirus Restrictions) (Wales) (Amendment) (No. 5) Regulations 2020, and the Health Protection (Coronavirus, Restrictions) (England) (Amendment) (No. 3) Regulations 2020, applicable in Wales and England respectively. These are covered in more detail below, and in later chapters.

At the time, in 24 March 2020, the President set out that the Stay at Home Rules had made the general position clear, which was that it was no longer permitted for a person, and this would include a child, to be outside their home for any purpose other than essential shopping, daily exercise, medical need or attending essential work.

What About Child Contact Arrangements? Is There an Exception?

The Government guidance was issued alongside the Stay at Home Rules on 23rd March 2020, which dealt specifically with child contact arrangements. It stated that 'Where parents do not live in the same household, children under 18 can be moved between their parents' homes.' The President stated that this *'establishes an exception to the mandatory 'stay at home' requirement; it does not, however mean that children must be moved between homes. The decision whether a child is to move between parental homes is for the child's parents to make after a sensible assessment of the circumstances, including the child's present health, the risk of infection and the presence of any recognised vulnerable individuals in one household or the other.'*

Parents Need to Communicate With Each Other

The President has set out that the best way to deal with these difficult times will be for parents to communicate with one another about their worries, and what they think would be a good, practical solution. Many people are very worried about Coronavirus and the health of themselves, their children and their extended family. Even if some parents think it is safe for contact to take place, it might be entirely reasonable for the other parent to be genuinely worried about this.

There Can Be Temporary Varation of the Cao – but Only by Agreement

The President has set out that where parents, acting in agreement, exercise their PR, to conclude that the arrangements set out in a CAO should be temporarily varied, they are free to do so. It would be sensible for each parent to record such an agreement in a note, email or text message sent_

What if There Is No Agreement to Temporarily Vary?

In cases involving intractable contact disputes, many family practitioners reading this book, will appreciate that sometimes, there will be no agreement to temporarily vary the child arrangements order. What is to happen here? The President has stated that where parents do not agree to vary the arrangements set out in a CAO, but one parent is sufficiently concerned that complying with the CAO arrangements would be against current PHE/PHW advice, then the President has set out that the parent may exercise their PR, and vary the arrangement to one that they consider to be safe. The guidance goes onto provide that if, after the event, the actions of a parent acting on their own in this way are questioned by the other parent in the Family Court, the court is likely to look to see whether each parent acted reasonably and sensibly in the light of the official advice and the Stay at Home Rules in place at that time, together with any specific evidence relating to the child or family.

What About Alternative Arrangements?

The President has set out that where, either as a result of parental agreement or as a result of one parent on their own varying the arrangements, a child does not get to spend time with the other parent as set down in the CAO, the courts will expect '**alternative arrangements**' to be made to establish and maintain regular contact between the child and the other parent within the Stay at Home Rules, for example remotely – by Face-Time, WhatsApp Face-Time, Skype, Zoom or other video connection or, if that is not possible, by telephone.

What Is the Key Message by the President?

In this guidance, the President has emphasised that the key message should be that, where Coronavirus restrictions cause the letter of a court order to be varied, the spirit of the order should nevertheless be delivered by making safe alternative arrangements for the child.

What Has Happened Since?

Since this guidance was issued on the 24 March 2020, we have of course seen some more easing of the social distancing restrictions across England and Wales. In England for example, there was some easing on 13 May 2020, and then in both England and Wales, there was a further easing 1 June 2020. However, even with the amended regulations that came into effect on 1 June 2020, there is still the provision for permitting contact as set out below. Firstly, in Wales, the Health Protection (Coronavirus Restrictions) (Wales) (Amendment) (No. 5) Regulations 2020, as of 1 June 2020, set out, at regulation 8 (1), that during the emergency period, no person may, without reasonable excuse, leave the area local to the place where they are living or remain away from that area, without reasonable excuse. Regulation 8 (2) gives various examples of 'reasonable excuse' including, in subparagraph (o), in relation to children who do not live in the same household as their parents, or one of their parents, continue existing arrangements for access to, and contact between, parents and children. For the purposes of this paragraph, 'parent' includes a person who is not a parent of the child, but who has parental responsibility for, or who has care of, the child.

In England, there are similar provisions contained in the Health Protection (Coronavirus, Restrictions) (England) (Amendment) (No. 3) Regulations 2020, which, as of 1 June 2020, set out that references to a 'parent' of a child as to include any person who is not a parent of the child, but who has parental responsibility for, or who has care of, the child, and for these purposes, a 'child' is a person under the age of 18. Regulation 6 (1) provides that no person may, without reasonable excuse, stay overnight at any place other than the place where they are living, and regulation 6 (2) sets out that the circumstances in which a person has a reasonable excuse. This includes cases where, in subparagraph (f), the person is a child that does not live in the same household as their parents, or one of their parents, and the overnight stay is necessary to continue existing arrangements for access to, and contact between, parents and children.

HOW WILL THE 24 MARCH 2020 GUIDANCE BE RELIED UPON IN SUBSEQUENT COURT HEARINGS?

It remains to be seen, that once we are firmly out of lockdown, and courts are able to resume back to normal, in so far as is possible, there will possibly be some backlog of court hearings to deal with. It may be that there will be a proliferation of cases, with the non-resident parent taking the children's case back before the court for enforcement of child arrangements. The parent may be doing so on the basis that the parent with care relied upon the Covid-19 pandemic, to unilaterally, vary the child arrangements, but the complaint by the applicant may be that in doing so, the resident parent acted irresponsibly, and inappropriately. We may possibly get many cases being brought, possibly determined through live evidence, on questioning whether a resident parent was appropriate in unilaterally varying the child arrangements during the lockdown. It is respectfully submitted that those of you who are representing family law clients at this stage, need to ensure that you are firmly advising on the very useful guidance given by the President, and in particular as the President has emphasised, '***… If, after the event, the actions of a parent acting on their own in this way are questioned by the other parent in the Family Court, the court is likely to look to see whether each parent acted reasonably and sensibly in the light of the official advice and the Stay at Home Rules in place at that time, together with any specific evidence relating to the child or family….***'

In my view, the parent with care will clearly need to be in a position to justify their decision making. In particular, there may well be questions as to what have they done to minimise the disruption in the child arrangements during this time? Have they offered other forms of contact in the meantime, such as video and/or telephone contact for example? If not, why not?

Reasonableness of 'Indirect Contact'?

The President's Guidance states that where it is felt that there is a need to vary the arrangements, the parties concerned are expected to consider alternative arrangements, so as to not establish, but to maintain regular contact child and the other parent. There is the specific reference to the methods utilised, such as remote methods of communication, including FaceTime, WhatsApp, Skype, Zoom and other video, and if this is not possible, by telephone. Many of us as who are family practitioners, will have used some, if not all of these methods, for the purposes of communication, whether in our professional or personal lives, and again here, when it does come to enforcement, I would suggest that the court will want to know how flexible the parent with care was in offering these alternative facilities? It is possible that the parent with care may rely upon the fact that they simply did not have a mobile or home phone available, with sufficient data, add-ons, a dongle, or access to a Wi-Fi signal, so as to enable this to be done. It may well be the case that the onus will be on the person who has not permitted contact to take place, to show, more likely than not, why they did not put into place, the necessary steps to ensure that indirect contact could occur.

By way of conclusion, it can therefore be seen that there may be potentially a lot of litigation coming out of the current pandemic as a result of child arrangements. This remains to be seen further.

CHAPTER TWO
PUBLIC FUNDING IN FAMILY CASES, DIGITILISATION AND THE IMPACT OF COVID-19

INTRODUCTION

As a family law practitioner, I have spent many years in advising and assisting clients who may be eligible for public funding. A lot of paperwork goes with providing such a service, which often entails making sure that you are on top of the paperwork, applications are submitted to the Legal Aid Agency in time, and that the necessary and up to date evidence is available, so as to provide the necessary evidence for eligibility in terms of means and merits.

DEVELOPMENTS IN FAMILY LAW PUBLIC FUNDING

Over the years, we have had a huge change in the way in which public funding is administered and available in family law cases. Gone are the days when we had 'green form legal aid' back in the early 1990's. You will be aware of the significant changes that came about in April 2013, as a result of the Legal Aid, Sentencing and Punishment of Offenders Act 2012 (LASPO).

The Legal Services Commission was renamed the Legal Aid Agency, and it became part of the Ministry of Justice. The Community Legal Advice was renamed Civil Legal Aid. The Funding Code Criteria and Procedures were replaced by the procedure and merits regulations.

In terms of the 'merits test', the funding requirement for seeking proceedings was originally set out under paragraph 12 of Part 1, Schedule 1 Legal Aid, Sentencing and Punishment of Offenders Act 2012 (LASPO). This set out the 'domestic violence' exception, whereby, under paragraph 12(1), it must have been shown that there had been, or there was a risk of, domestic violence between the one person and the other, and the one person was, or at risk of being the victim of that domestic violence. In such a case, the person who had been subjected to, or was subject to the risk, would be entitled to public funding for the family dispute. The initial definition of domestic violence for the purposes of LASPO was set out as ***'any incident of threatening behaviour, violence or abuse (whether psycho-logical, physical, sexual, financial or emotional) between individuals who are associated with each other.'***

The Civil Legal Aid (Procedure) (Amendment) Regulations 2014 amended the Civil Legal Aid (Procedure) Regulations 2012, and when these came into effect, they provided that an application for civil legal services described in Paragraph 12 of Part 1 of Schedule 1 to the Act must include evidence of the domestic violence or the risk of domestic violence. For the purpose of this, the evidence of domestic violence or risk of domestic violence was to be provided in one or more of various forms. This included, and was not limited to some of the following type of evidence:

(a) a relevant unspent conviction for a domestic violence offence;

(b) a relevant police caution for a domestic violence offence given within the twenty four month period immediately preceding the date of the application for civil legal services;

(c) evidence of relevant criminal proceedings for a domestic violence offence which had not concluded;

(d) a relevant protective injunction which was in force or which was granted within the twenty four month period immediately preceding the date of the application for civil legal services;

(e) an undertaking given in England and Wales under section 46 or 63E of the Family Law Act 1996 (or given in Scotland or Northern Ireland in place of a protective injunction) -

(i) by the individual ("B") with whom the applicant for civil legal services ("A") was in a family relationship giving rise to the need for the civil legal services which were the subject of the application; and

(ii) within the twenty four month period immediately preceding the date of the application for civil legal services, provided that a cross-undertaking was not given by A;

(ea) evidence that B was on relevant police bail for a domestic violence offence

We then saw the implementation of The Civil Legal Aid (Procedure) (Amendment) Regulations 2016 No. 516. The Procedure Regulations were amended, so that for regulation 33(2) (supporting documents: domestic violence), there were then changes in terms of the evidence of domestic violence or risk of domestic violence that must be provided. These amendment regulations of 2016 allowed for the evidence of domestic abuse to go back to 5 years (60 months). Also, as for financial abuse, the Legal Aid Agency had stated that they would have discretion to consider such abuse. This could include looking at bank statements, e-mails, texts between the parties to demonstrate financial abuse. We then saw further changes on the 8 January 2018, when The Civil Legal Aid (Procedure) (Amendment) (No. 2) Regulations 2017 came into effect. These had the effect of updating the Civil Legal Aid (Procedure) Regulations 2012, in so far as regulations 33 (supporting documents: domestic violence) and regulation 34 (supporting documents: protection of children) are concerned, so that this 2017 Statutory Instrument removed the time limit upon the evidence that could be accepted. Regulation 2(3) of this 2017 instrument also removed the time limit of twenty-four months for certain types of evidence of child abuse, or risk of child abuse. The instrument provided that the evidence requirements would be met if an applicant provided one or more new forms of evidence.

WHAT WERE THE ADDITIONAL FORMS OF EVIDENCE THAT THE LEGAL AID AGENCY WOULD ACCEPT?

The additional forms of evidence introduced included:

- evidence provided by a domestic violence support organisation that had provided support related to the applicant's needs as a victim of domestic violence;

- evidence that the applicant had been granted indefinite leave to remain under the domestic violence provisions in the Immigration Rules;

- evidence from a person acting on behalf of a local housing authority;

- evidence from an independent domestic violence advisor; and

- a letter from a public authority where domestic violence had been identified

The Instrument therefore broadened the categories of health professionals who could provide evidence, to include a registered medical practitioner or health professional registered with a relevant regulator body.

WHAT ARE THE CURRENT PRACTICAL DIFFICULTIES IN LIGHT OF COVID-19?

Despite the relaxation of the criteria for eligibility for public funding in family cases, as of 8 January 2018, it has nonetheless still required the necessary documentary evidence to be available. This has continued to take the form of quite often letters from GPs, documentation from the police, information from local authorities and housing departments. How has this gathering of information, been impacted by Covid-19, and how has Legal Aid Agency been able to assist in this regard?

There has been recent guidance provided by the Legal Aid Agency, insofar as the practical steps of gathering the necessary information. This guidance applies across England and Wales.

EMERGENCY CERTIFICATES

Coronavirus (COVID-19): Legal Aid Agency contingency response

For full details, see the link: https://www.gov.uk/guidance/coronavirus-covid-19-legal-aid-agency-contingency-response#legal-aid-agency-ways-of-working

It is of note that the Legal Aid Agency (LAA) have extended the time limit of emergency certificates to 12 weeks. A wider scope limitation will be granted appropriate to the proceedings, and the cost limit extension is now to £2500.

What About the Evidence Requirements?

Coronavirus (COVID-19): working with clients

For full details, see the link: https://www.gov.uk/guidance/coronavirus-covid-19-working-with-clients

In relation to domestic abuse and child abuse, and the evidence requirements, the LAA have now expanded how domestic violence requirements may be evidenced to make it easier for victims of abuse to access public funding during the pandemic stage. These changes give as much flexibility as possible within the existing legislation. The LAA have provided that as of 9 April 2020, the followings changes have applied to the guidance in relation to evidence of both domestic violence and child abuse:

- removing the need for evidence to be submitted on letter headed paper where required
- allowing additional evidence types to be submitted via email
- allowing solicitors to provide an email documenting that they have spoken to a member of the police, and received confirmation that the perpetrator did receive a caution for a domestic violence/child abuse offence, or that the perpetrator was involved in ongoing criminal proceeding relating to a domestic abuse/child abuse offence

What About Assessing Financial Eligibility Where a Client Cannot Attend the Premises?

The LAA 'Coronavirus (COVID-19): working with clients' document referred to above, sets out that it is now possible, in certain situations, to assess means, without accompanying evidence, where it is not practicable to do so. It provides that where a client is staying at home, it may still be possible to collect evidence by email or post. Reasonable efforts to collect evidence should still be made and recorded before assessing without evidence, if that is not possible.

What About Digital Signatures?

The LAA 'Coronavirus (COVID-19): working with clients' document referred to above, sets out that digital client signatures will be acceptable as an alternative to handwritten ('wet') signatures and will meet the contract requirements.

The LAA have confirmed that text messages are not considered an acceptable method of digital signature, and are not covered by the Law Society. If it is not possible to directly obtain a client signature, the LAA advice is as follows:

- One should make a note on the file, explaining why this was the case, countersigned by a supervisor.
- One should also make a note on the relevant form itself.
- The legal representative would also need to provide express evidence (for example email exchanges or telephone attendance notes) demonstrating that the client formed the appropriate intention to sign and submit the application form, or showing that the legal representative had been directly appointed by a court or tribunal to act for the client.
- To avoid delays or issues with processing, the legal representative should seek a signature at the earliest possible opportunity. If they are unable to secure a client signature (including a digital signature), where it is clear that reasonable attempts have been made to secure the client's

signature, and there has been evidence of the client's intention to sign the form, or that the legal representative has been appointed to act for a client by a court or tribunal, then they may still submit a claim.

Means Eligibility for Public Funding

The LAA 'Coronavirus (COVID-19): working with clients' document referred to above, sets out where an applicant's financial position changes, the LAA will exercise discretion in allowing more time for the applicant to provide evidence relating to the change in financial circumstances. The LAA will also exercise discretion when considering the evidence provisions surrounding expenditure incurred by the applicant.

WHAT IS THE POSITION WITH FACE TO FACE MEDIATION?

The Civil Legal Aid (Procedure) (Amendment) Regulations 2020 came into force on the 15th May 2020. These regulations have amended the Civil Legal Aid (Procedure) Regulations 2012, in relation to applications for determinations that an individual qualifies for civil legal services under sections 9 and 10 of the Legal Aid, Sentencing and Punishment of Offenders Act 2012. Some key aspect of these changes are as follows:

- Regulation 4 omits the definition of face-to-face provider in regulation 2 of the Procedure Regulations.

- Regulation 7 amends regulation 61 of the Procedure Regulations to set out circumstances when an individual applying for family mediation need not attend the provider's premises in person. The reader will see that that is a very important amendment, so as to enable a client to still get the benefit of family mediation, but in light of the pandemic, to avoid the need to attend the mediator's premises.

- Regulation 8 amends Schedule 1 to the Procedure Regulations to expand further the types of evidence of domestic violence which may support an application for civil legal services under paragraph 12 of Part 1 of Schedule 1to the Act.

CONCLUSION

In this chapter, we have seen that there have been huge developments in the administration and provision of the public funding in family law over the years. Given the current pandemic, the Legal Aid Agency have ensured that those who are in need of vital and necessary public funding, are still able to receive this, with the necessary safeguards in place to reduce the spread of the infection.

CHAPTER THREE
DEVELOPMENTS IN THE FAMILY PROCEDURE RULES

INTRODUCTION

Over the last few years, there has been various inroads made in so far as the move towards increased digitalisation. We have seen this in not just areas of family law, but also in other areas, such as in private client, where we have seen a move towards online inheritance tax form completions and probate applications. In the field of family law, there has been a lot of movement towards digitalisation, and such advancements, in hindsight, have proved beneficial, not only in allowing practitioners to work more efficiently, but also, now, in light of the pandemic, to allow for less physical contact and use of paper, and therefore in reducing the risk of spreading the infection. What are the various schemes that have been set up in family law areas towards greater digitalisation? We will consider the various Pilot Practice Directions that have been set up over the years below.

PILOT PRACTICE DIRECTION 36Q

This PD came into effect on 23rd of April 2020. It ends on 30 October 2020. This has changed PD12B (Child Arrangements Programme). The effect of this pilot is that it is still possible to apply for child arrangements orders, and to enable such applications to be progressed during the pandemic. Paragraph 1.1 particular provides that there is a need to ensure that the administration of justice is carried out, in such a way as to not endanger public health, and take account of available resources.

PILOT PRACTICE DIRECTION 36M

This came into effect on 31 January 2019. It ends on 31 August 2020. This pilot came in at a stage before we had the onset of the Covid-19 pandemic, and it illustrates the family courts' movement towards the online systems. This particular practice direction permits applications for care, supervision, and certain other applications under the Children Act 1989, to be filed and processed online. There are a number of conditions which need to be met before the pilot will be utilised, notably that access to the online system must be permitted, that the application needs to be started in the family court, and the process provided for the online system is to be completed.

AMENDMENTS TO PRACTICE DIRECTION 17A

This came into effect on 23rd of April 2020. PD 17A currently provides for confirmation as to which documents are to contain the statement of truth. It will be known that since the Family Procedure Rules 2010 have been in place, many of the previous documents we had, which had to be sworn or affirmed, now contain the statement of truth instead. This includes for example, the statement in support for the application for a divorce, and the Form E, to enable one to pursue an application for a financial order. Given the pandemic, there have been further amendments to PD17A, so that those documents which require a statement of truth, and therefore are to be 'signed', such a signature can now incorporate an electronic signature. This would be applicable where the online application process allows for an electronic signature. We have already seen this with Pilot Practice Direction 36M above, whereby paragraph 5.2 of this PD provides that the applicant must file with the court, an application, which includes the name of the person who the online system requires to sign a statement of truth, recorded against the statement of truth.

PILOT PRACTICE DIRECTION 36P

This PD came into force on 9th March 2020. This pilot will end on the 31 January 2021. It relates to placement applications and the online system. This Practice Direction supplements rule 36.2 FPR 2010 (transitional arrangements and pilot schemes), and it allows: (a) for applications in placement proceedings, and all required accompanying documents, to be filed with the court via uploading them to the online system; and (b) for applications, judgments and orders in such proceedings to be served by the court via the online system. This PD applies where all of the following conditions are met:

(a) the application is in placement proceedings,

(b) access to the online system for filing via uploading such applications and all required accompanying documents is permitted;

(c) the application is started in the family court; and

(d) the application and all required accompanying documents are filed in the period commencing 9 March 2020, and ending 31st January 2021.

PILOT PRACTICE DIRECTION 36G

This came into effect on 26 March 2018. It ends on 31 January 2021. This was another pilot that was set up a few years ago, so as to enable certain applications to be filled in, and filed through the online process. This relates to private children matters, and therefore applications under Section 8 Children Act 1989. The pilot required the application to be filled in online, and the applicant would then be expected to save or print the application, and then to file at court. It is worthy of note that for the purposes of the Mediation Information and Assessment Meeting (MIAM) requirements, paragraph 4.1 of this pilot requires that the application must include from the prospective applicant, confirmation that they have attended a MIAM, or that they are relying on a MIAM exemption, or confirmation that a mediator's exemption applies. As set out in paragraph 6.1, this pilot also makes provision for the name of the person to whom the online system requires to sign the statement of truth, to be printed underneath the statement of truth.

PRACTICE DIRECTION 36N

This came into effect on 27 May 2020. This pilot ends on 30 September 2020. It covers the procedure for online filing and progression of certain applications financial remedy under Part 9 FPR 2010. The requirements for this pilot to be used are that there needs to be an application for a financial remedy in connection with an application for a matrimonial order, or the notice of intention to proceed financial remedy must have been made, the application must not be for a consent order, the applicant must be legally represented, access to the online system must permitted, and finally, the application must have started in the family court. Just like for Pilot Practice Direction 36G, there are similar provisions relating to claiming any MIAM exemption.

PRACTICE DIRECTION 36L

This pilot came into effect on 14 January 2019. The pilot ended on 5 April 2020. This pilot set out the procedure for using the online system in relation to the various stages of applications for a matrimonial order. It applies where the application is for a matrimonial order, where there is sought, a decree of divorce. The PD applies when an individual seeks to use the online system, as long as the application does not become defended (in which case it would need to exit the scheme), and as long as the application started in the family court.

Linked with this, it is also worthy of note, that recently, there has been guidance issued by Her Majesty's Courts and Tribunals Service (HMCTS), dated May 2020. This is called ***'Detailed guide to submitting a case on the system'***, and is the updated guidance on submitting a divorce online. It also assists legal representatives, where they can submit a divorce application without a marriage certification under certain circumstances. They need to provide supporting evidence for the reasons why, with a covering letter/application. The guidance is available in full at the following link: https://assets.publishing.service.gov.uk/government/uploads/system/uploads/attachment_data/file/883855/Submitting_a_Case_-_May_2020.pdf

GUIDANCE FROM THE JUDICIARY

In the Remote Access Family Court Guidance, provided by Mr Justice MacDonald (Version 4, dated 16 April 2020) and available at the following link: https://www.judiciary.uk/wp-content/uploads/2020/04/The-Remote-Access-Family-Court-Version-4-Final-16.04.20.pdf, there are some significant aspects surrounding digitalisation in light of the pandemic. Note the following aspects in particular:

IS A 'WET' SIGNATURE NECESSARY FOR DOCUMENTS?

At paragraph 5.2.2 of this guidance, His Lordship has set out that some courts have rejected applications for decree nisi, draft finance consent orders and other documents because they did not have a 'wet' signature on them. On 27 March 2020, the President of the Family Division made clear that the rules do not indicate that a 'wet' signature is a procedural requirement and that, from now, 'wet' signatures are not a requirement for applications, consent orders, etc and such documents are not to be rejected by courts on that basis.

WHAT IS THE POSITION WITH CHILD ARRANGEMENTS ORDERS APPLICATIONS?

At paragraph 5.2.3 of this guidance, His Lordship has stated that applications for child arrangement orders continue to be processed during the COVID-19 pandemic. Wherever possible, parents and legal representatives should use the online child arrangements service to avoid delay. If the matter is urgent, such as if a hearing is needed within 3 days, or there are serious safety concerns, the online service should not be used and contact should be made with the local court. Where a parent or legal representative is not eligible to use the online service, and the matter is not urgent, paper C100 applications should be sent.

WHAT IS THE POSITION WITH E – BUNDLES?

This guidance provides some vital assistance in this regard. At paragraph 5.7, His Lordship has stated that the ability of the judge and the parties to access an electronic bundle for the hearing comprises an essential element of an effective remote hearing. Therefore, the wholesale move to remote hearings as a result of the COVID-19 pandemic means ensuring the availability of e-bundles and the software packages to use them effectively is a matter of extreme urgency. His Lordship has set out that the use of a paper bundle is not only incompatible with a remote hearing, but also presents a potential avenue of transmission of the virus.

WHAT DOES THE FPR PROVIDE ON E - BUNDLES?

There is specific reference to the Family Procedure Rules 2010, PD27A, para 2.5. This allows the use of e-bundles in a hearing before a High Court judge with that judge's permission, and in other cases as have been approved by the Designated Family Judge for the relevant area, with the agreement of the President of the Family Division and in accordance with the local arrangements. In financial remedies work, Mostyn J has issued Financial Remedies Courts – e-bundles protocol dated 3 March 2020, which provides for the use of e-bundles in financial remedies cases.

CONCLUSION

It is difficult to imagine any positive consequences of the impact of the pandemic, given the devastating effect that Covid-19 has had and continues to have on people's lives, health, families, businesses and aspirations. However, given that we have all had to embrace using technology more widely, the onset of the pandemic has strengthened the argument for making more use of digitalisation, even once the lockdown is fully lifted. After all, one may argue that if a divorce can now be progressed fully 'online', which saves, a lot of time, effort and material, why should we go back to what it was like beforehand? The 'Lockdown' has shown that we can efficiently do a lot more online, and even for some service users, who may not be as confident with technology as others are, given the support and guidance that is provided in using technology, the emerging move towards greater digitalisation may reduce their pessimism.

CHAPTER FOUR
DOMESTIC ABUSE, SOCIAL DISTANCING AND COVID-19

INTRODUCTION

One of the inevitable consequences of the current lockdown, is that many families are spending greater time at home, and, although this does have its obvious benefits, in terms of reducing the strain on the NHS for example, and reducing the spread of the infection, there are also hidden dangers, such as the possibility of increased domestic abuse within the household. Furthermore, even if clients are able and willing to come forward for support and guidance relating to domestic abuse, what are the practical steps in being allowed to attend court, and pursue orders for personal protection? These and other matters will be considered in this chapter.

GIVEN THE CURRENT LOCKDOWN, WHEN IS A VICTIM OF ABUSE PERMITTED TO LEAVE THE HOUSE?

ENGLISH REGULATIONS

Consider the Health Protection (Coronavirus, Restrictions) (England) (Amendment) (No. 3) Regulations 2020. These are dated 1 June 2020, and amend the Health Protection (Coronavirus, Restrictions) (England) Regulations 2020. The Regulations prohibit anyone leaving the place where they live without reasonable excuse, and these regulations have continued to be updated as the Government has continued to relax the social distancing restrictions further.

WHAT IS REASONABLE EXCUSE CURRENTLY DEFINED AS?

Regulation 6 (1) provides that no person may, without reasonable excuse, stay overnight at any place other than the place where they are living. Regulation 6 (2) sets out that the circumstances in which a person has a reasonable excuse. The key provisions in regulation 6(2) to bear in mind for cases involving domestic abuse, it is suggested, are the subparagraphs set out below. The salient provision is contained in regulation 6 (2)(d), which permits one to stay overnight at any place other than the place where they are living, where it is reasonably necessary for the person to stay elsewhere, so as to (iv)to avoid injury or illness, or to escape a risk of harm; (v)to obtain medical assistance. Also, regulation 6 (2) provides that the person is permitted to stay elsewhere: (e) to fulfil a legal obligation or participate in legal proceedings; (g) where the person is unable to return to the place where the person lives, because (i)it is not safe for the person to live there, (ii) the person may not lawfully travel there, or is required by law to stay in another place.

WHAT ABOUT SOCIAL GATHERINGS?

Regulation 7 (1) provides that during the emergency period, unless paragraph (2) applies, no person may participate in a gathering which takes place in a public or private place (a)outdoors, and consists of more than six persons, or (b)indoors, and consists of two or more persons. In regulation 7 (2), there is reference to the fact that this paragraph applies, amongst others, (vi)to enable one or more persons in the gathering to avoid injury or illness or to escape a risk of harm. Regulation 7 (3) provides that for the purposes of this regulation (a)there is a gathering when two or more people are present together in the same place in order to engage in any form of social interaction with each other, or to undertake any other activity with each other.

WELSH REGULATIONS

Consider the Health Protection (Coronavirus Restrictions) (Wales) (Amendment) (No. 5) Regulations 2020. These are dated 1 June 2020 also, and amend the Health Protection (Coronavirus Restrictions) (Wales) Regulations 2020. Just like the English regulations have provided, these Welsh regulations, at regulation 8 (1), provide, amongst others things, that during the emergency period, no person may, without reasonable excuse leave the area local to the place where they are living or remain away from that area.

WHAT IS REASONABLE EXCUSE CURRENTLY DEFINED AS?

Regulation 8 (2) sets the provisions out. The relevant provisions, in cases involving domestic abuse, it is suggested, are the various sub-paragraphs as follows:

(c) seek medical assistance, including accessing any of the services referred to in paragraph 42 of Schedule 1 or accessing veterinary services;

(l) meet a legal obligation, including attending court or satisfying bail conditions, or to participate in legal proceedings;

(m) access or receive critical public services, including (ii) social services; (iii) services provided by the Department for Work and Pensions; (iv) services provided to victims (such as victims of crime or domestic violence);

(r) avoid injury or illness or escape a risk of harm.

WHAT DOES NOT CONSTITUTE REASONABLE EXCUSE?

Regulation 8 (3) describes this as it not being a reasonable excuse for a person to leave the area local to the place where the person is living to do something, or remain away from the area to do something, if it would be reasonably practicable for them to do that thing within the area.

WHAT ABOUT GATHERING WITH OTHERS?

Regulation 8 (5) covers this. It provides that during the emergency period, no person may participate in a gathering outdoors except in certain cases, most notably, under subparagraph (d), which states where the gathering is necessary to (iv) to participate in legal proceedings, or fulfil a legal obligation.

WHAT ORDERS ARE CURRENTLY AVAILABLE FOR PERSONAL PROTECTION?

Non-Molestation Orders

These are covered by s.42 Family Law Act 1996 (FLA 1996). These are used to prevent a respondent from molesting the applicant or a relevant child. Non- Molestation orders can be made not only by application, but also by courts own motion in any family proceedings to which the respondent is a party.

Occupation Orders

These are covered by ss.33-41 Family Law Act 1996 (FLA 1996). Occupation orders are 'draconian' in nature. Thus, are harder to obtain than a non- molestation order.

WHAT ARE THE MAIN CATEGORY OF APPLICANT?

There is the list of associated persons, set out in ss. 62 – 63 FLA 1996. Some of the key applicants are:

(a) People who have been or are still married to each other, or are or have been civil partners

(b) Cohabitants or former co-habitants

(c) Relatives. This include, as set out in s. 63 (1) FLA 1996 as:

- the father, mother, stepfather, stepmother, son, daughter, stepson, stepdaughter, grandmother, grandfather, grand-daughter or grandson of a person against whom an order is sought or that person's spouse or former spouse,

- the brother, sister, uncle, aunt, niece or nephew of a person against whom an order is sought or that person's spouse or former spouse,

- if the parties are cohabitants, any person who would have been included in either of the above categories and had been married

(d) People who live, or have lived in the same household, otherwise than merely by reason of one of them being the other's employee, tenant, lodger or boarder.

(e) People who have agreed to marry one another, whether or not that agreement has been terminated.

(ea) They have or have had an intimate personal relationship with each other which is or was of significant duration

(f) People who in relation to a child are a parent of that child or have or have had parental responsibility for that child.

(g) Are parties to the same family proceedings.

It will be seen that in the family law context, the list of associated persons is such that it will incorporate many domestic situations, Given the restrictions to social distancing, how does the law offer protection for such persons, particularly in emergencies?

Section 45(1) FLA 196 provides that without notice orders may be made where the court considers it just and convenient to do so. The court must consider all the circumstances, including:

1. Any risk to the applicant or a relevant child attributable to the respondent if the order is not made immediately

2. Whether it is likely that the applicant will be deterred or prevented from pursuing the order if it is not made immediately

3. Whether the respondent appears to be evading service and that the applicant or child will be seriously prejudiced by any delay in service.

WILL THE COURTS HEAR 'WITHOUT NOTICE' APPLICATIONS DURING THE LOCKDOWN?

Many family practitioners will have experienced carrying out the necessary steps in seeking a 'without notice' order, most notably a without notice non-molestation order. From my experience, this may involve instructions been provided at short notice, having to put together a statement in support, in a very limited time, completing the application form (FL401), sorting out eligibility for public funding if necessary, contacting the court, lodging the application, attending court, making the application, arranging service, and advising the client throughout. I am sure that those of you who have applied for such orders on behalf of clients will agree with me that such applications involve a lot of work being done in a short period of time, and although such applications can be mentally exhausting, given the nature of the application, they are absolutely necessary to provide essential and immediate protection. In light pandemic, there are a number of inevitable questions associated with such applications. In particular, can courts continue to hear such applications during the lockdown, what if you and/or your client cannot physically get to court, and can a remote hearing be used for 'without notice' applications? In this regard, the guidance from Sir Andrew McFarlane, President of the Family Division and Head of Family Justice, in COVID 19: National Guidance for the Family Court, dated 19 March 2020, is of significance here. At paragraph 8 of this guidance by the President, His Lordship has set out that remote hearings are also suitable for injunction applications where there is no evidence that is to be heard (or only limited evidence). In my submission, I would suggest that the President has in his mind, in stating this, that this covers both 'without notice', and in fact, some limited 'return date' hearings for injunctions for personal protection. Furthermore, at paragraph 13 of the Guidance, the President has set out even where a case is urgent, it should be possible for arrangements to be made for it to be conducted remotely. The President has said that where a case is genuinely urgent, and it is not possible to conduct a remote hearing, and there is a need for pressing issues to be determined, then the court should endeavour to conduct a face-to-face hearing in circumstances, in terms of the physical arrangement of the court room and in the waiting area, which minimise the opportunity for infection.

Remote Hearings in the Family Justice System: A Rapid Consultation

Nuffield Family Justice Observatory (Nuffield FJO) – May 2020

On the 14 April 2020, the President of the Family Division announced a two-week rapid consultation on the use of remote hearings in the family justice system to be undertaken by the Nuffield Family Justice Observatory. The observatory sought to gather evidence from families with children and all professionals working in the family justice system, including judges, barristers, solicitors, Cafcass workers, court staff and social workers. The consultation was until the 28th April 202, to then enable the President to receive a summary of the responses by end April, with a view to issuing further guidance. The consultation report can be accessed via the following link: https://www.nuffieldfjo.org.uk/news/1000-respondents-rapid-consultation-remote-hearings.

In the context of domestic abuse cases, this report has highlighted that where coercive control is a factor in a relationship, there is a risk that the remote court process, can in itself be used as a coercive control tactic.

What other steps are currently being taken in relation to the development of the law surrounding domestic abuse, and particularly, to provide assistance to those who are vulnerable? There is currently going through Parliament, the Revised Domestic Abuse Bill 2020.

REVISED DOMESTIC ABUSE BILL 2020

This Revised Bill was reintroduced in the New Parliament, by starting in the House of Commons, on 3 March 2020. Covid-19 has had some impact on the Bill progressing swiftly. Amongst other matters, the Bill brings about some changes to matters relating to Participation Directions and the Cross Examination.

PARTICIPATION DIRECTIONS

The Family Procedure (Amendment No. 3) Rules 2017 came into force on 27th November 2017. Part 3A FPR 2010 covers Vulnerable Persons and Special Measures. In particular, rule 3A.4 provides that the court must consider whether a party's participation in the proceedings (other than by way of giving evidence) is likely to be diminished by reason of vulnerability and, if so, whether it is necessary to make one or more participation directions. Before making such participation directions, the court must consider any views expressed by the party about participating in the proceedings. In the Revised Domestic Abuse Bill, there is consideration of the proposals for legislative changes to consider the automatic eligibility for special measures in domestic abuse cases, removing the burden on the victim to prove they are in fear or distress.

CROSS EXAMINATION BY ALLEGED PERPETRATOR IN CHILDREN CASES

Consider the case of *PS v. BP [2018] EWHC 1987 (Fam).* This case involved an application by the father for a child arrangements order, to be able to see his child. Given that the mother had raised allegations of domestic abuse, which involved allegations of rape and attempted strangulation, the court decided to list the matter for a finding of fact hearing, pursuant to PD12J. At this hearing, the trial judge refused to allow the father, who was a litigant in person, to cross examine the mother as to her allegations, and instead the judge sought for the father to provide the questions to the judge, who in turn, would put these to the mother. The appeal was in relation to the issues surrounding allowing a litigant in person to cross-examine the alleged victim.

In the Revised Bill of March 2020, the Government have extended the automatic ban on cross-examination in person in the family courts in England and Wales and provided for appropriate scrutiny of the Domestic Abuse Commissioner by the National Assembly for Wales. There was the joint committee report on the draft Domestic Abuse Bill, **(SESSION 2017-19, HL PAPER 378 / HC 2075: DRAFT DOMESTIC ABUSE BILL)**. It is available at the following link: https://assets.publishing.service.gov.uk/government/uploads/system/uploads/attachment_data/file/869947/CCS207_CCS0120992896-001_CP_214_Web_Accessible.pdf

This report was presented to Parliament by the Secretary of State for the Home Department by Command of Her Majesty March 2020. In this report, the Select Committee raised the concern as to the potential for inconsistency in applications, because too many victims of domestic abuse would be protected only at the discretion of the court. The committee recommend that the mandatory ban was extended, so that it applied where there are other forms of evidence of domestic abuse, as in the legal aid regime threshold. The Government has accepted the Committee's recommendation. The Government intends to broadly replicate the evidence criteria set out in regulations under the public funding regime. The Government will also retain the discretionary prohibition, to ensure that judges are still able to prohibit cross-examination in person in any other case where they feel it is necessary.

CHAPTER FIVE
REMOTE HEARINGS, FAMILY LAW AND COVID-19

INTRODUCTION

The reader will be aware that for many family law practitioners, a typical week could involve conducting several court hearings, interviewing clients, drafting documents and attending several types of meetings at various locations. These tasks will often involve a lot of travelling. Up until recently, we all no doubt had an established routine in place, in terms of making sufficient time for the journey to court and back, being familiar with public transport timings, remembering to charge the laptop, remembering to take the work phone, as well as other devices and documents to court. We would all be familiar with the court staff, the judiciary, other lawyers, professionals and clients. All this routine that we have all come to accept and repeat, without question, has changed as a result of the current pandemic, and we have all had to learn new ways of trying to carry out the same job. This has not only been physically challenging, in terms of, setting up appropriate working practices in our own family homes, but it has also required us to mentally adapt, and face new challenges, in terms of still being able to advise and represent our respective clients appropriately, and to be able to follow cases through just as efficiently, if not better, than what we did before the lockdown. This chapter will consider the guidance that has been handed down by the senior judiciary in running remote hearings, and I will also consider some key themes coming out of the leading case law authorities.

COVID 19: NATIONAL GUIDANCE FOR THE FAMILY COURT

This guidance, dated 19 March 2020, was handed down by Sir Andrew McFarlane, President of the Family Division and Head of Family Justice. It is available at the following link:

https://www.judiciary.uk/announcements/covid-19-national-guidance-for-the-family-court-message-from-president-of-the-family-divison/

At paragraph 4, the President had set out for the time being, all Family Court hearings should be undertaken remotely either via email, telephone, video or Skype, etc (remote hearing], where the requirements of fairness and justice require a court-based hearing, and it is safe to conduct one, then a court-based hearing should take place.

The reader should note that in terms of the Family Procedure Rules 2010, these do allow for the use of remote hearings in appropriate cases. In particular, r 1.4(e) FPR 2010 provides that the court must further the overriding objective by making use of technology. Also, r 4.1(3)(e) FPR 2010 provides that the court may hold a hearing and receive evidence by telephone or by using any other method of direct oral communication.

WHAT TYPE OF CASES ARE SUITABLE FOR REMOTE HEARINGS?

At paragraph 8 of this guidance, the President has set out that the following categories of hearing are suitable for a remote hearing:

- All directions and case management hearings;

- Public Law Children hearings, involving Emergency Protection Orders, Interim Care Orders and Issue Resolution Hearings

- Private Law Children hearings, involving First Hearing Dispute Resolution Appointments, Dispute Resolution Appointments, other interim hearings, and simple short contested cases

- Injunction applications where there is no evidence that is to be heard (or only limited evidence).

- Financial Cases – reference to the guidance issued for the Financial Remedies Court by Mostyn J on 17 March 2020 at Appendix B

- Appeals.

- Other hearings as directed by the judge concerned

Also, it is possible that other cases may also be suitable to be dealt with remotely. This will need to be determined on a case-by-case basis. The President has emphasised that where a case cannot be listed for a remote hearing, then any existing listing should be adjourned, and the case must be listed promptly for a directions hearing, which should be conducted remotely.

WHO HAS TO ARRANGE THE HEARING?

At paragraph 16, the President has set out that the responsibility for making technical and other arrangements for a remote hearing and for confirming the details of the arrangements for the hearing to the other parties no later than 24 hours prior to the remote hearing taking place is to be undertaken by the following party liaising with the court:

- The local authority in a public law case
- The applicant, if legally represented, in a private law case
- The respondent, if legally represented and, where the applicant is not, in a private law case
- The court where no party is legally represented

WHAT DO YOU NEED TO FILE IN ADVANCE?

At paragraph 18, the President has set out that the day before the hearing, the applicant must electronically file a PDF bundle, which complies with FPR PD27A, and which in any event must include, as a minimum:

- A case summary and chronology;
- The parties' positions statements
- The previous orders that are relevant to the remote hearing
- All essential documents that the court requires to determine the issues that fall for determination at the remote hearing
- A draft order
- Completed advocates' forms together with the single address that the signed and sealed forms are to be returned to for distribution to the advocates

Remote Access Family Court Guidance – Version 4 (16 April 2020)

This guidance, (at the time of writing, it being Version 4, dated 16 April 2020), has been provided by Mr Justice MacDonald. It is available at the following link: https://www.judiciary.uk/wp-content/uploads/2020/04/The-Remote-Access-Family-Court-Version-4-Final-16.04.20.pdf

His Lordship has set out that the aim of this document is to identify the current problems which arise from the urgent need to move to a default position of remote hearings, to identify potential solutions to those problems, and to set out operational protocols to govern the position whilst further solutions are being arrived at. As solutions are found to each problem, updated versions of this document will be circulated. There is reference in this Volume 4, to the fact that on the 9 April 2020, the Lord Chief Justice, Master of the Rolls and the President of the Family Division issued a communication to the judiciary setting out some indicators that may assist the allocated judge in deciding whether, in his or her discretion, a particular hearing should be heard remotely, and if so what form of remote hearing should be adopted. That communication does not amount to official guidance and is not intended to be directive.

LEGAL AID AGENCY GUIDANCE ON REMOTE HEARINGS AND PAYMENTS

There has been recent guidance provided by the Legal Aid Agency, insofar as the payment and timings of remote hearings. This is set out in the publication by the Legal Aid Agency (LAA), entitled ***'Remote Family Hearings: updated ways of working in light of the significant increase in remote family hearings'*** Version 2, and is dated 15 April 2020. For full details, see the link: https://assets.publishing.service.gov.uk/government/uploads/system/uploads/attachment_data/file/879645/LAA-FAS-updatev2.pdf

This document sets out the how the Family Advocacy Scheme (FAS) operates during the pandemic, and will be updated on a regular basis as further issues emerge.

WHAT ARE THE LEADING CASE LAW AUTHORITIES IN RELATION TO REMOTE HEARINGS AND FAMILY LAW DURING THE CURRENT PANDEMIC?

I will consider the essentials of the following leading cases in turn:

Re P (A Child: Remote Hearing) [2020] EWFC 32

A (Children) (Remote Hearing: Care and Placement Orders) [2020] EWCA Civ 583

Re B (Children) (Remote Hearing: Interim Care Order) [2020] EWCA Civ 584

Re Q [2020] EWHC 1109 (Fam)

Padero-Mernagh v Mernagh (Divorce- Nullity- Remote Hearing) [2020] EWFC 27

Re P (A Child: Remote hearing) [2020] EWFC 32

This was a family court decision, handed down on the 16 April 2020, by Sir Andrew McFarlane (President of the Family Division). The care case was heard remotely. The matter had been listed for a planned 20-day hearing in April 2020. It was a composite hearing, where findings were sought of Fabricated Induced Illness (FII) and determination of the care plan. The timing of the hearing was affected by the Covid-19 pandemic. At that pre- hearing review on the 3 April 2020, all the parties, including the judge, were of the view that the hearing would go ahead, as planned, on the 20 April, albeit remotely, following the guidance given by Mr Justice MacDonald on the conduct of remote hearings which gave an account [at paragraph 2.2.1] of a number of remote hearings that had been successfully accomplished in the early days following the lockdown. The President stated at paragraph 8, that it seemed that those involved in the case, read that advice as indicating that all hearings must now proceed as remote hearings and at the hearing on the 3 April, the discussion during the hearing was about how the remote hearing would be conducted, and not whether it should be heard remotely. His Lordship said that if that was the understanding of MacDonald J's document, it was a misunderstanding. MacDonald J's document was firmly aimed at the mechanics of the process; it did not offer guidance, let alone give direction, on the wholly different issue of whether any particular hearing should, or should not, be conducted remotely. Establishing that a hearing can be conducted remotely, does not in any way mean that the hearing must be conducted in that way. There was no application to adjourn the hearing on the basis that there should not be a remote hearing. The court however, heard an application for the hearing to be postponed on the basis that the mother had unfortunately contracted the Covid-19 virus infection herself and would not be fit to take part in the court process. The judge did not accede to that application at that stage, but indicated that the mother's health and her ability as a result of her health to engage in the court process would be kept under review. Arrangements went ahead for the compilation of an electronic bundle, and for the hearing to be set up to be undertaken over the Skype for Business platform.

The President stated at paragraphs 11 -12, that this type of hearing seemed to be well outside the categories of hearing which could be contemplated as being appropriate for remote hearings before the

Family Court. FII is a category of case is a particular form of child abuse which requires exquisite sensitivity and skill on the part of the court. His Lordship stated that these type of hearing are a particularly unusual cases and, from a judge's perspective, it is a crucial element in the judge's analysis for the judge to be able to experience the behaviour of the parent who is the focus of the allegations throughout the oral court process; not only when they are in the witness box being examined in-chief and cross-examined, but equally when they are sitting in the well of the court and reacting, as they may or may not do, to the factual and expert evidence as it unfolds during the course of the hearing. His Lordship was surprised that this hearing was planned to go ahead as a remote hearing. The trial judge was invited by the President to consider adjourning the hearing so that it would be re-listed once the lockdown requirements had been removed and it could be heard in the ordinary way at a full oral hearing. His Lordship was of the view that the hearing had to be adjourned.

WHAT FACTORS ARE TO BE TAKEN INTO ACCOUNT IN HAVING A REMOTE HEARING?

The President stated at paragraph 24, that the decision as to whether to hold a remote hearing in a contested case involving the welfare of a child is a particularly difficult one for a court to resolve. A range of factors are likely to be in play:

- The need to maintain a hearing in order to avoid delay and to resolve issues for a child in order for her life to move forward is likely to be a most powerful consideration in many cases, but it may be at odds with the need for the very resolution of that issue to be undertaken in a thorough, forensically sound, fair, just and proportionate manner.

- The decision to proceed or not may not turn on the category of case or seriousness of the decision, but upon other factors that are idiosyncratic of the particular case itself, such as the local facilities, the available technology, the personalities and expectations of the key family members and, in these early days, the experience of the judge or magistrates in remote working.

- It is because no two cases may be the same that the decision on remote hearings has been left to the individual judge in each case, rather than making it the subject of binding national guidance.

The President stated at paragraph 26, that it was simply impossible to contemplate a final hearing of this nature, where at issue are a whole series of allegations of factitious illness, being conducted remotely. His Lordship took the view that a trial of this nature was simply not one that could be contemplated for remote hearing during the present crisis.

A (Children) (Remote Hearing: Care and Placement Orders) [2020] EWCA Civ 583

This case was the first appeal in a case relating to the welfare of children to reach the Court of Appeal on the issue of remote hearings during the COVID 19 pandemic. The President of the Family Division handed down the leading judgment in the Court of Appeal on the 30 April 2020. Some key aspects in the case were as follows:

WHAT FACTORS WILL INFLUENCE THE COURT AS TO WHETHER TO HAVE THE HEARING REMOTELY?

These were set out in paragraph 9 of the judgment, and will include the following:

i. The importance and nature of the issue to be determined; is the outcome that is sought an interim or final order?

ii. Whether there is a special need for urgency, or whether the decision could await a later hearing without causing significant disadvantage to the child or the other parties;

iii. Whether the parties are legally represented;

iv. The ability, or otherwise, of any lay party (particularly a parent or person with PR) to engage with and follow remote proceedings meaningfully. This factor will include access to and familiarity with the necessary technology, funding, intelligence/personality, language, ability to instruct their lawyers (both before and during the hearing), and other matters;

v. Whether evidence is to be heard or whether the case will proceed on the basis of submissions only;

vi. The source of any evidence that is to be adduced and assimilated by the court. For example, whether the evidence is written or oral, given by a professional or lay witness, contested or uncontested, or factual or expert evidence;

vii. The scope and scale of the proposed hearing. How long is the hearing expected to last?

viii. The available technology; telephone or video, and if video, which platform is to be used. A telephone hearing is likely to be a less effective medium than using video;

ix. The experience and confidence of the court and those appearing before the court in the conduct of remote hearings using the proposed technology;

x. Any safe (in terms of potential COVID 19 infection) alternatives that may be available for some or all of the participants to take part in the court hearing by physical attendance in a courtroom before the judge or magistrates.

The President stated that although each case must be determined in the light of its own specific factors, here, the appeal would be allowed against the judge's decision to conduct the remote hearing of proceedings which included applications for placement orders. The decision was wrong to hear it. His Lordship emphasised that this decision does not mean that there can be no remote final hearings on an application for a care order or a placement for adoption order.

NEED TO BE CAUTIOUS IF ONLY PARTIES TO ATTEND COURT ARE LAY PARTIES

At paragraph 58, the President set out that there is a need for caution, when the only witness(es) required to attend court are the lay parties when others, for example the key social worker, are not. When a lay party is required to attend court, but his or her advocate is not, the cause for concern at the imbalance in the process must be heightened. Consideration must be given to the potentially exposed position of a witness giving live evidence in front of a judge in the absence of his or her lawyers or any of the other parties and in response to questions asked over a video link.

WHAT IF PARTIES OPPOSE A REMOTE HEARING?

At paragraph 61, the President set out that if all parties oppose a remotely conducted final hearing, this is a very powerful factor in not proceeding with a remote hearing. Whilst here, the Children's Guardian did not oppose proceeding with the planned hearing, all of the other parties, including the local authority did. In such circumstances, when the applicant local authority itself did not support a remote contested final hearing, a court would require clear and cogent reasons for taking the contrary view and proceeding to hold one.

Re B (Children) (Remote Hearing: Interim Care Order) [2020] EWCA Civ 584

In this case, the President of the Family Division handed down the leading judgment in the Court of Appeal, also on the 30 April 2020. This was appeal relating to an interim order that had been made. The appeal was allowed. The interim car order was set aside. The appeal concerned a 9-year-old boy, who, as result of the order made, was removed from the care of his grandmother, and placed in foster care. At paragraph 34, the Court of Appeal took the view that this was a classic case for an adjournment, so that a considered decision could be taken about removal, if indeed that option was going to be pursued after reflection. An adjournment would have enabled the parties and the court to have all the necessary information.

REMOTE HEARINGS OVER THE PHONE VERSUS VIDEO PLATFORM?

At paragraph 35, the court took the view there is a qualitative difference between a remote hearing conducted over the telephone and one undertaken via a video platform. Whilst it may have been the case that the provision of video facilities was limited at the particular court at the time of the hearing, it was now the case that the option of using a video link is much more widely available. Where that is the case, a video link is likely at this time to be the default option in urgent cases.

Re Q [2020] EWHC 1109 (Fam)

The President of the Family Division handed down the judgment in case, at the High Court, on the 6 May 2020. This case involved an appeal from a case management decision made by a judge, via a remote hearing. It related to long-running private law proceedings concerning a child, aged 6. The appeal was allowed. There had been a psychological report, which recommended for there to be a change of primary carer from mother to father. Following receipt of the expert report, the court directed that contact should be further increased so that the child was spending alternate weeks with each parent. That arrangement had continued through the current lockdown. The father sought for a switch of residence in his favour, which mother opposed. The contested matter had been set down for a final hearing on 22 April 2020, for 3 days, to be conducted remotely.

THE WAY FORWARD?

The President stated that in light of the Guidance that has been issued and the decisions handed down by the Court of Appeal in relation to remote hearings, each judge or magistrate must consider the individual case before the court and determine whether or not it should proceed remotely in whole or in part.

Padero-Mernagh v Mernagh (Divorce- Nullity- Remote Hearing) [2020] EWFC 27

This was a family court judgment, handed down by Mr Justice Williams on the 3 April 2020. The case illustrates how well remote hearings can run. In the case, the petitioner wife had lodged an application for divorce, in relation to her marriage, which had taken place. The respondent husband filed an Acknowledgement of Service and a 'Reply/defence'. The husband started that the marriage was bigamous, because the wife remained married to another man which took place previously. The husband had cross- petitioned for nullity. Both parties, for the most part, represented themselves in the proceedings. The husband's case was that the marriage was void ab initio on the basis that the petitioner had contracted a previous undissolved marriage, and the marriage certificate indicated a ceremony in circumstances other than those set out by the petitioner in her evidence. The petitioner had admitted that a ceremony took place, but denied that it constituted a marriage valid.

Remote Hearing Took Place Due to The Coronavirus Pandemic

The matter was listed for a 3-day hearing, which was expected to take place at the Family Court sitting, on the 30 March 2020. The development of the coronavirus pandemic intervened. His Lordship considered that it was likely that a fair hearing could be achieved remotely. The parties had previously expressed a wish for the matter to be concluded as quickly as possible. Arrangements were made for the hearing to be conducted remotely by Skype for business. The 30th March was set aside for reading and for testing the Skype facility. The hearing itself was to take place on 31 March, with 1 April being set aside for judgment writing. Testing of the Skype link took place successfully on 30 March. The hearing was scheduled and convened by the clerk, who ensured that all the parties were online before the judge joined the hearing. At the commencement of the hearing, the judge set out the ground rules that he expected to be followed during the course of the remote hearing in order to ensure that each party was able to give evidence, make submissions and participate to the fullest extent possible.

Remote Hearing Ran Satisfactorily

At paragraph 14, His Lordship set out that apart from minor technical glitches and occasional interruptions by the respondent, the hearing proceeded in accordance with the directions. All involved abided in the main by the ground rules. His Lordship was of the view that both the wife and husband were satisfied that the remote hearing had allowed them to put their cases and give their evidence in a fair way.

CONCLUSION

We can see from the above cases that have been handed down so far, that as each case is decided, more and more useful guidance is being provided, not only as to the use of remote hearings, but how they are to operate, going forward. The guidance provided by Justice McDonald will continue to be updated, and no doubt, we will continue to receive further developments as new issues come to light. One thing is for sure, and that is, the court system has had to adapt very quickly, to enable the successful running of remote hearings, and this will continue to progress.

CHAPTER SIX
PUBLIC CHILDREN AND ADOPTION LAW CASES AND IMPACT OF COVID-19

INTRODUCTION

In this chapter, I will consider the impact of the pandemic to the effective running of public children cases, and consideration of those matters whereby local authorities are involved. I will consider in particular, the recent changes to the regulations, particularly as to how they relate to adoption processes and procedures, fostering and care planning.

WHAT ARE THE CHANGES TO THE PRIMARY LEGISLATION AND REGULATIONS IN ENGLAND?

The Adoption and Children (Coronavirus) (Amendment) Regulations 2020

These regulations came into force on 24th April 2020. These regulations will cease to have effect on the 25th September 2020, and they apply to England only. These regulations provide amendments to various regulations, so as to relax and amend the requirements, with a view to assisting the children's social care sector during the coronavirus pandemic. Some key aspects of these will be covered below, and will involve looking at specifically:

- ADOPTION
- CARE PLANNING

- FOSTERING
- PRIVATE FOSTERING

CHANGES TO ADOPTION

Briefly, the changes are:

- Removal of the duty on adoption agencies to refer cases to the adoption panel
- Amendments to the adopter approval process,
- To enable information that currently has to be collected during stage 1 of the approval process to be collected during stage 2,
- To relax some timescales within which adoption agencies must take steps.

There are several changes to various aspects of the original and amended Adoption Regulations over the years.

PANELS AND CONSTITUTION

In the Adoption Agencies and Independent Review of Determinations (Amendment) Regulations 2011, there is provision in regulation 4 (1), that the adoption agency must constitute one or more adoption panels, as necessary, to perform the functions of an adoption panel. This is now changed, so that (a)in paragraph (1) for ***'must constitute'*** it is now substituted ***'may constitute'*** Also, at paragraph (2) of these regulations, the Adoption Agency must ensure that an adoption panel has sufficient members, and that individual members have between them the experience and expertise necessary to effectively discharge the functions of the panel. This is now changed, so that in paragraph (2), there is omitted, the words *'that an adoption panel has sufficient members'*

In The Adoption Agencies (Panel and Consequential Amendments) Regulations 2012, there was provision for the fact that in a case where the Agency was considering whether the child ought to be placed for adoption, and (b)either paragraph (2A) or paragraph (2B) applied, the Agency was not to refer the case to the adoption panel. Paragraph (2A) applied where: (a)the child was placed for adoption by the adoption agency, or was being provided with accommodation by them, (b)no adoption agency was authorised to place the child for adoption, and (c)the child had no parent or guardian, or the agency considered that the conditions in section 31(2) of the 1989 Act were met in relation to the child. Paragraph (2B) applied where (a) an application had been made, and had not been disposed of, on which a care order might be made in respect of the child, or (b)the child was subject to a care order, and the adoption agency were not authorised to place the child for adoption. For these cases, there is still no need to take the child's case to adoption panel. However, paragraph (2C) provided that in a case not falling within paragraph (2), the adoption agency was to send the information and reports referred to in paragraph (2D) to the adoption panel. Those practitioners who specialise in adoption cases will know that this relates to cases where children have been relinquished for adoption by the parent (s) with parental responsibility. The 2020 Regulations relax this provision, so that paragraph (2C) is now replaced with, *'(2C) in a case not falling within paragraph (2), the adoption agency must decide whether to: (a)require the case to be referred to an adoption panel, or (b)proceed to make a decision under regulation 19 without such a referral, and where the case is to be referred to the adoption panel, the adoption agency must send the information and reports*

referred to in paragraph (2D) to the adoption panel.' It is submitted that this will only be applicable to the relinquished baby cases, as only those would have been referred to adoption panel. Therefore, as from 24 April 2020, the Adoption Agency can decide whether to refer to Adoption Panel, or can now proceed to decide that the child ought to be placed from adoption under Regulation 19 (AA Regulations 2005), without the need to go to panel. If it does still decide to take the child's case to adoption panel, there is still a need to send the requisite documents to adoption panel.

REVIEWS AND ADOPTION

In the Adoption Agencies Regulations 2005, regulation 36 provided that where an adoption agency is authorised to place a child for adoption, but the child is not for the time being placed for adoption, the agency must carry out a review of the child's case(a)not more than 3 months after the date on which the agency first had authority to place; and (b)thereafter not more than 6 months after the date of the previous review, until the child was placed for adoption. This is now relaxed, so that it now reads:

> ***(A1) Subject to paragraph (B1) an adoption agency does not have to carry out a review required by this regulation where the adoption agency decide that it is not reasonably practicable to carry out the review of the child's case.***
>
> ***(B1) Paragraph (A1) does not apply where the adoption agency is satisfied that a review is necessary to safeguard and promote the welfare of the child.***

CHANGES TO CARE PLANNING

Briefly, the changes are:

- Amendment of the Care Planning, Placement and Case Review (England) Regulations 2010.
- It is possible for a person to be approved as a local authority foster carer for a temporary period (not just a person who is a relative, friend or person connected to the child), and there is the extension as to the length of that period from 16 to 24 weeks.
- An increase as to the length of time a foster carer can be approved as an emergency foster carer to 24 weeks.
- A number of timescales within which local authorities must take steps are also relaxed.

DEFINTION OF CONNECTED PERSONS

In the Care Planning, Placement and Case Review (England) Regulations 2010, regulation 2 (interpretation), there is now omitted the definition of '***connected person***'. Until the 24 April 2020, this was defined as a relative, friend or other person connected with the child.

TEMPORARY APPROVAL OF PERSONS

The revised regulation 24 reads that where the responsible authority is satisfied that the most appropriate placement for the child is with a person who has not yet been approved as a local authority foster parent, they may approve that person as a local authority foster parent for a temporary period not exceeding 24 weeks, provided that they first comply with the requirements of paragraph (2).

It should be noted by the reader therefore, that the previous 16 weeks temporary approval has now become 24 weeks, and also the reference to ***'connected person'*** has gone. The rest of regulation 25 remains, and hence, the local authority can now extend the 24 weeks for a further 8 weeks, taking it to 32 weeks.

POSITION WITH HOW VISITS ARE TO BE CONDUCTED

Previously, regulation 28 provided that as part of their arrangements for supervising the child's welfare, the local authority was to ensure that the representative visited the child in accordance with this regulation, wherever the child was living. The frequency of the visits is to continue, as set out in regulation 28, but there is now inserted, the following provision:

> ***(1A) any visit required by this regulation may be conducted by telephone, video-link or other electronic means.***
>
> ***(1B) Where R is unable to visit the child within the timescales set out in this regulation the responsible authority must ensure that R visits the child as soon as is reasonably practicable thereafter.***

I would suggest to the reader that this is a major issue for local authorities in England to bear in mind

POSITION WITH TIMING OF THE 6 MONTH REVIEW

Previously, with the position regarding ***'looked after reviews'***, these were to be conducted, so that the first review needed to be within 20 working days of the date on which the child became looked after, the 2nd review being not more than 3 months after the first, and subsequent reviews of not more than 6 months. This timescale is now relaxed, so that the words '***at intervals of not more than six months***' are now substituted with the words '***where reasonably practicable thereafter***'.

CHANGES TO FOSTERING

Briefly, these regulations:

- Amend the Fostering Services (England) Regulations 2011.
- They relax some timescales within which fostering agencies must take steps and remove the duty on fostering service providers to refer cases to the fostering panel.

CONSTITUTION OF FOSTERING PANELS

Regulation 23 of the Fostering Services (England) Regulations 2011 required the fostering service provider to maintain a list of persons who are considered by them to be suitable to be members of a fostering panel. In particular, reg 23(4) required that the fostering service must constitute one or more fostering panels, as necessary, to perform the functions of a fostering panel. This regulation has now become relaxed, so that in reg23(4), the words '***must constitute***' are changed to '***may constitute.***' Also, regulation 24 required that no business may be conducted by a fostering panel unless at least the following met as the panel: (i)either the person appointed to chair the panel or one of the vice chairs, (ii)one member who is a social worker who has at least three years' relevant post-qualifying experience, and (iii) three, or in the case of a fostering panel established under regulation 23(5) four, other members. This regulation has now become relaxed, so that in 24(1)(iii) (meetings of fostering panel), there is now substituted, the words *'(iii)one other independent person'*

FOSTERING PANELS

Regulation 27(2)(b) of the Fostering Services (England) Regulations 2011 required that a fostering service provider must not approve X as a foster parent unless (a)they have completed their assessment of X's suitability, and (b)the fostering panel has considered the application. This is now relaxed, so that it now reads at the in reg 27(2)(b) at the beginning ***"where the case was referred to the fostering panel,"***

CHANGES TO PRIVATE FOSTERING

They relax timescales within which local authorities must take steps.

ACTION FOLLOWING NOTIFICATION

Regulation 4 of the Children (Private Arrangements for Fostering) Regulations 2005 provided that where a local authority had received notification, they were to arrange for an officer of the authority within seven working days to (a)visit the premises where it was proposed that the child would be cared for and accommodated; (b)visit and speak to the proposed private foster carer and to all members of his household; (c)visit and speak to the child, alone unless the officer considered it inappropriate; (d)speak to and, if it is practicable to do so, visit every parent of or person with parental responsibility for the child; and (e)establish such matters listed in Schedule 2 as appeared to the officer to be relevant. This is now relaxed, so that the reference to *'seven working days'* is changed to or *'as soon as is reasonably practicable'*

Also, Regulation 7 provided that where a local authority had received a notification under regulation 5 or 6, they needed to arrange for an officer of the authority within seven working days to (a)visit the premises where the child is being cared for and accommodated; (b)visit and speak to the private foster carer and to all members of his household. This is now relaxed, so that the reference to *'seven working days'* is changed to or *'as soon as is reasonably practicable'*

In conclusion, this chapter has shown that the Adoption and Children (Coronavirus) (Amendment) Regulations 2020 have had an important impact on ensuring the effective running of adoption and fostering services during the pandemic.

CHAPTER SEVEN
DEPARTMENT OF EDUCATION GUIDANCE FOR CHILDREN'S SOCIAL CARE DEPARTMENTS IN ENGLAND

INTRODUCTION

The Covid-19 pandemic has inevitably led to local authorities across England and Wales having to adapt to the social distancing restrictions, but at the same time, to ensure that they are not compromising in any way, their statutory duties towards children and families. How are social workers to carry out statutory visits, how does one comply with court directed orders, what has changed insofar as panels are concerned, and how are families and children to be reassured during these difficult times? These, and other questions will be considered in this chapter. I will consider the guidance has been recently provided by the Department of Education for England in this chapter.

GUIDANCE FOR CHILDREN'S SOCIAL CARE SERVICES IN ENGLAND

The Department of Education Guidance provided updated guidance on the 6 May 2020 referred to as 'Coronavirus (COVID-19): guidance for children's social care services'

This can be accessed following the link: https://www.gov.uk/government/publications/coronavirus-covid-19-guidance-for-childrens-social-care-services/coronavirus-covid-19-guidance-for-local-authorities-on-childrens-social-care.

This Guidance of 6 May 2020 relates to amendments that have been made to the April 2020 Guidance, to provide for extra flexibility in some circumstances.

SUMMARY OF KEY ASPECTS OF THE GUIDANCE

WHAT IS THE POSITION WITH CHILD PROTECTION CONFERENCES?

The reader will be aware that those people who would often be attending a child protection conference (CPC) would be the parents, social services staff who may have undertaken an assessment of the child, other family members, foster carers and other professionals involved, such as perhaps the school, the police, legal representatives and perhaps the NSPC. The conference process is significant in assisting the process of deciding whether the child is suffering or at risk of suffering significant harm. If the child comes in such a category, an inter-agency Child Protection Plan will be prepared at the Case Conference. The conference will decide whether the child should continue to be subject to a child protection plan. Given the vital functioning of child protection conferences, how do these go ahead in the current pandemic? In answer to this, the Department of Education has set out in this guidance that multi-agency working is crucial to ensuring the protection of vulnerable children, and multi-agency child protection conferences should therefore go ahead, using video conferencing or conference calling solutions where appropriate.

WHAT IF FAMILIES REFUSE ENTRY TO A SOCIAL WORKER, PARTICULARLY IF THE FAMILY ARE SELF ISOLATING?

The Guidance provides that if children and families are anxious about infection risks if the social worker visited, then the worker should explain why it is essential that they have access to the home, or that they see and speak to the children, to ensure they are safe and well. It does not need to always be a face-to-face visit, but it should be sufficient to reassure the social worker that the child is not currently at risk of harm and that their welfare is safeguarded. The general duties on a local authority under s.17 Children Act 1989, in relation to safeguarding and promoting the welfare of children in need in their area remain unchanged. S.47 Children Act 1989 remains, in terms of investigating cases where the local authority has cause to suspect that a child is or is likely to suffer significant harm. The guidance specifically provides that if a family refuses access, and there is a risk to the life of the child or a likelihood of immediate serious harm, the local authority should follow the immediate child protection procedures set out in ***Working Together to Safeguard Children – A guide to inter-agency working to Safeguard and Promote the Welfare of Children*** (July 2018, and updated in February 2019). This is available at the following link: https://www.gov.uk/government/publications/working-together-to-safeguard-children--2#history

WHAT SUPPORT IS TO BE PROVIDED TO CHILDREN WHO HAVE A SOCIAL WORKER?

The Guidance provides that multi-agency support should continue, with appropriate flexibility in how this is delivered, such as via telephone, or online support, rather than face-to-face meetings, where it is risk-assessed as safe to do so. A local authority needs to be conscious of reduced protective factors from abuse and neglect available to children and families and increased stressors as a result of coronavirus (COVID-19), and work with local safeguarding partners to ensure continuity and consistency of support.

WHAT IS THE POSITION WITH COMPLIANCE WITH ORDERS FOR CONTACT RELATING TO A CHILD IN CARE?

Some key principles set out in the Department of Education Guidance are that:

- There is an expectation that contact between children in care and their birth relatives will continue.
- It is essential for children and families to remain in touch at this difficult time.
- Contact arrangements should be assessed on a case by case basis taking into account a range of factors, including the government's social distancing guidance and the needs of the child.
- Where it may not be possible, or appropriate, for the usual face-to-face contact to happen at this time and keeping in touch will, for the most part, need to take place virtually.
- Where face-to-face contact is not possible, the guidance encourages social workers and other professionals to reassure children that this position is temporary, and will be reviewed as soon as it is possible to do so.

The Guidance states that it is expected that the spirit of any court-ordered contact in relation to children in care to be maintained, and social workers need to determine how best to support those valuable family interactions based on the circumstances of each case. It can be seen that this ties with the guidance given by the President of the Family Division, in relation to Child Arrangements and Contact, dated 24 March 2020, and referred to in Chapter One in this book.

WHAT IS THE POSITION WITH FOSTERING PANELS AND ASSESSMENTS?

The Department of Education Guidance provides that the local authority needs to ensure that assessments and approvals are thorough, and comply with regulations, but the DfE do not want these to be unnecessarily delayed. It is stated that there is already sufficient flexibility for fostering services to convene remote panels. Some key aspects set out by DfE are as follows:

- To assist with the process, in light of increasing demand, and where places are required more urgently, the Fostering Services (England) Regulations 2011 have been amended to minimise any delays.

- It is now optional to refer applications for potential foster carers, ongoing suitability assessments of existing foster carers, and any cases where a foster carer is not deemed suitable, to a fostering panel for a recommendation.

- In cases where panel meetings are conducted, the number of people required to be part of the panel meeting has been reduced to allow for likely staff shortages during this time.

- Panels can be conducted remotely.

- The DfE still expect a panel to be convened (making use of remote meetings and the flexibility provided around panel numbers), but where a panel cannot be convened, approval can take place without a panel. The DfE would not expect this to be the norm.

- Also, foster carers can now be assessed and approved without unnecessary delay. Regulation 26 of the 2011 regulations has been amended, so that the fostering service provider does not need to wait for health information, or the DBS (criminal record) checks to be completed, in order to continue with their assessment of suitability of the prospective foster carer and their household. The requirement for health information to be provided by prospective foster carers has not been removed altogether, but the requirement for it to be supported by a medical report has been. This now allows fostering service providers to accept self-reported medical information.

- The DfE still expects the local authority to continue to seek formal medical reports as soon as reasonably practicable. These changes clarify that the assessment process can continue to the second stage, whilst awaiting medical information and DBS (criminal record) checks.

- Before making a final decision approving a person as suitable to foster, the fostering service will still need to have the medical information and DBS checks, along with the other information specified in Schedule 3 of the regulations.

WHAT IS THE POSITION WITH REVIEWS, GIVEN ISSUES WITH STAFF SHORTAGES AND ILLNESS?

The Department of Education Guidance states that it is still expected that a local authority will conduct visits and regular reviews of children's care plans, which may be virtually. As we saw in the previous chapter, there have been changes to the Care Planning, Placement and Case Review (England) Regulations 2010, so that:

- Regulation 28 – This has been amended, to allow visits to be conducted as soon as reasonably practicable where these visits cannot be made within the defined timescales. It has also been amended to allow these visits to be conducted by telephone, video-link or other electronic means.
- Regulation 33 – This has been amended, so that the local authority is still required to review the child's case within 20 working days of the date on which the child becomes looked after, and to carry out the second review not more than three months after the first. However, for third and subsequent reviews, these reviews are to be carried out when reasonably practicable.
- A review must still be carried out if any of the criteria for a review in regulation 33(3) of the same regulations are met, or in certain circumstances, where the child requests a review.

WHAT IS THE POSITION WITH PRIVATE FOSTERING?

As we saw in the previous chapter, there have been changes to the regulations relating to private fostering in England. The Department of Education have amended some of the timeframes to the Children (Private Arrangements for Fostering) Regulations 2005, so as to provide more time for visits to take place during the coronavirus (COVID-19) pandemic period. The regulations had previously provided for the initial visits to planned, or existing private fostering arrangements to take place within 7 days of the local authority becoming aware of the of such arrangements. These regulations have been amended, so that the visit needs to take place within 7 days or as soon as reasonably practicable, to allow for flexibility where it is not possible to conduct the visit within 7 days. There is also flexibility in the maximum interval between visits during the pandemic period – currently every 6 weeks in the first year, and every 12 weeks thereafter. The local authority is to keep clear records, so as to set out the reasons for not being able to comply with the usual time limits.

SOME CHANGES TO ADOPTION PROCESSES

ARE ADOPTION PANELS TO BE CURRENTLY USED FOR MATCHING AND APPROVALS?

As we saw in the previous chapter, there have been changes to adoption processes. Some key aspects set out by Department of Education are as follows:

- The DfE have removed the requirement to have an adoption panel.
- The DfE encourage the use of virtual panels
- The changes have allowed the Adoption Agency more flexibility, so as to reduce the constitution of panels, and of cases going to panels.
- The requirement to hold a central list remains.

This chapter has considered the guidance that has been provided by the Department of Education in relation to England. In the next chapter, I will consider the Welsh government's Guidance for Wales.

CHAPTER EIGHT
WELSH GOVERNMENT GUIDANCE FOR CHILDREN'S SOCIAL CARE DEPARTMENTS IN WALES

I will begin this chapter by considering some recent changes in so far as how the adoption assessment process operates in Wales, and there will then be a consideration of the guidance for children's social services in Wales provided by the Welsh Government in light of the current pandemic.

ADOPTION AGENCIES (WALES) AMENDMENT) REGULATIONS 2020

There have been some recent changes brought about by the Adoption Agencies (Wales) Amendment) Regulations 2020. These came into force on1 April 2020. These amend the Adoption Agencies (Wales) Regulations 2005, by inserting new regulations 19A and 20A into the 2005 regulations. What are the key provisions?

ADOPTION REGISTER FOR WALES FOR CHILDREN

New regulation 19A – This requires adoption agencies to refer to the Adoption Register for Wales (within the required timescale) details of children whom the adoption agency has been authorised to place for adoption.

WITNESSING OF THE S.19 AND S.20 ADOPTION AND CHILDREN ACT 2002 CONSENTS

New regulation 20A. This lists those persons authorised to witness the execution outside England and Wales of forms of consent to placement for adoption by parents and guardians and, as the case may be, to the making of a future adoption order. The previous regulation 20 of the 2005 regulations is amended, so that an adoption agency must request the appointment of a Welsh family proceedings officer, or an officer of CAFCASS to obtain consent from a parent or guardian to the placement or adoption of a child in their care only where the parent or guardian resides in England and Wales.

THE ADOPTION ASSESSMENT PROCESS TIMESCALES

These are now bringing this very much in line with the amendments to the English Adoption Agencies Regulations 2005, so that in summary, there is now a New Part 4 (regulations 21 to 30G) to the 2005 Regs. This now provides for a 2 - stage approval process for prospective adopters (the pre-assessment process – stage 1 and the assessment decision – stage 2). Also, new regulations 21 to 27 (stage 1) apply where a person has notified an adoption agency that they want to adopt a child and the agency has notified that person that it has decided to proceed with the pre-assessment process in respect of them. Furthermore, new regulations 28 to 30G (stage 2) apply where, following the adoption agency's decision that the prospective adopter may be suitable to adopt, the prospective adopter has notified the adoption agency within six months of that decision that they wish to proceed to stage 2 of the approval process.

WHEN MUST THE DECISION TO APPROVE AN ADOPTER BE MADE BY?

New regulation 27 provides that an adoption agency must decide in light of that information, whether the prospective adopter may be suitable to adopt a child. That decision must be made within two months from the date on which the adoption agency notified the prospective adopter that they had decided to proceed with the pre-assessment process in accordance with new regulation 21, but the agency may delay making that decision where it is satisfied that there are good reasons for doing so, or upon the request of the prospective adopter.

GUIDANCE FOR CHILDREN'S SOCIAL CARE SERVICES IN WALES

The Welsh Government has provided updated guidance on the 22 May 2020 referred to as 'Children's social services during the COVID-19 pandemic: guidance'

This can be accessed following the link: https://gov.wales/childrens-social-services-during-covid-19-pandemic-guidance-0

This guidance has updated the previous guidance of 21 April 2020, in light of the changes to the social distancing rules. I have summarised some aspects of the guidance below:

SOCIAL WORKERS CARRYING OUT VISITS

The 'Rules on Staying at Home and Away from Others' (the 'Stay at Home Rules') introduced by the UK Government on 23rd March were such that no one, including a child, should leave their home other than for essential shopping, daily exercise, medical need or attending essential work and school for those who continue to attend. There were then the amendments on the 7 April 2020, in relation to the 2-metre rule. The Welsh Guidance provides that this means that face to face contact arrangements for children is no longer advised, and safe alternative contact arrangements should be made. In the majority of cases, this means that face to face contact between social workers and families should be suspended. However, the Welsh Government emphasise that this does not mean that the frequency of contact with children, care leavers, families and carers should be reduced unless there are grounds to reduce the frequency of contact based on information about the care and support needs of the child. Social workers and social care staff should follow PPE guidance when visiting private households.

WHAT ABOUT MAINTAINING CONTACT BETWEEN ADOPTED AND FOSTERED CHILDREN AND THEIR FAMILIES?

The Welsh Government guidance stresses that one of the key principles of the Social Services and Wellbeing (Wales) Act 2014 and the Local Authority Fostering Service (Wales) Regulations 2018, is that there should be continued contact between the child and their family while the child is in the care of the local authority. The Welsh Government expects that alternative forms of contact between children in care and their birth relatives will continue. It is essential for children and families to remain in touch. Local authorities should consider ways in which equipment can be provided to families to enable continued contact. Contact arrangements should therefore be assessed on a case by case basis, taking into account a range of factors including the UK government's social distancing guidance and the needs of the child. It may not be possible, or appropriate, for the usual face-to-face contact to happen at this time and keeping in touch will, for the most part, need to take place virtually.

CHILD PROTECTION CONFERENCES

The Welsh Government recognises that capacity to review and update Care, Support and Protection Plans in the usual way may be impeded during the outbreak. However, a clear record of the decisions taken, any changes in level of risk and the response to these should be maintained.

WHAT ABOUT COURT ORDERED CONTACT AND ONGOING PROCEEDINGS?

The guidance provides that if there is court ordered contact, and contact is unable to take place or happens remotely, local authorities should record the reasons for their decisions. It is recognised that contact centres are currently closed. The guidance provides that where supervised contact arrangements are in place, consideration should be given to undertaking supervision using video conferencing in the home of the foster carer, with a staff member present during the video conference, where it is safe to do so, to maintain levels of supervision. If the family is self-isolating or being shielded, the staff member should be present remotely.

COMPLIANCE WITH ADOPTION AGENCIES (WALES) (AMENDMENT) REGULATIONS 2020

The Welsh Government has considered the implications associated with the introduction of the Adoption Agencies (Wales) (Amendment) Regulations 2020, and have provided assurance to providers that no action, whether by use of Ministerial Directions powers or otherwise, will take place in relation to any infractions of the requirements in the new Regulations between 1st April 2020 and 30th September 2020, or until normal running is resumed, whichever is the sooner, provided that these occur with good reason. This could mean in some circumstances, that agencies will run Stage 1 and Stage 2 processes concurrently, should they so wish. The requirement currently remains however, that all the necessary checks including health assessments and DBS checks need to be fully completed before an adopter is approved. This could mean for example that medical assessments are left until the end of the process.

ADOPTION PANELS

Th Welsh Government have provided that Regional and Voluntary Adoption Agencies should consider how panels can continue to ensure the adoption system continues to place children, but it is accepted that some delays may occur especially for the less straightforward cases. Panels should consider continuing remotely through video or conferencing calls. and this should be determined on a case by case basis. Adoptive parents and prospective adopters should only be asked to join via video/telephone calls.

OTHER MISCELLANEOUS PROVISIONS

- In relation to care and support plans, pathway plans and reviews, the Welsh Government provides that local authorities should make every effort to fully comply with the legislation during this emergency and continue to fully take into account the needs and wishes of children in their care.

- Whilst physical reviews meetings are not advised, Independent Reviewing Officers (IROs) should use digital means to carry out reviews, monitor progress and make decisions.

- The Welsh Government is confident that there is already sufficient flexibility within The Fostering Panels (Establishment and Functions) (Wales) Regulations 2018 for fostering services to convene remote panels.

- In relation to the undertaking of medical assessments for prospective foster carers, the Fostering Panels (Establishment and Functions) (Wales) Regulations 2018 set out a requirement that a fostering services provider should, as part of the assessment process for prospective foster carers, 'obtain details of health (supported by a medical report)'. To help the current situation, the Welsh Government have set out processes that are now available for Fostering Agencies to follow for the implementation of medical assessments.

- In terms of introductory meetings for children with new adopted parents, just like the Department of Education Guidance provides for England, the Welsh Government have taken the view that there should not be a blanket ban in this regard. There needs to be a case by case, risk-based decision.

- With regard to carrying out Adoption Medicals, the Guidance provides that there is sufficient flexibility within existing arrangements to allow agencies to operate safely. The interim measure which was introduced in April 2020, allows agencies to run Stage 1 and Stage 2 of the two-stage adoption assessment process to run concurrently during the crisis.

- In regards to care leavers, the guidance provides that local authorities should continue to meet statutory duties, including offering personal advisers to care leavers and preparing or reviewing pathway plans using innovative ways. Personal advisers should use their judgment to determine the

> nature of their contact with the young people they work with during this period. Personal advisers are encouraged to use technology to contact young people through phone or video, to minimise the need for face-to-face contact.

In this chapter, we have seen that, just like the Department of Education have done for England, the Welsh Government have provided some very welcome and necessary guidance on the safe and effective running of adoption, fostering and children's services during the current situation.

FINAL POINTS

I am sure that you will agree that a vaccine for Covid-19 cannot come soon enough. Whatever the form any vaccine takes, there will be many discussions over its availability, its target group, cost, and no doubt, it's side effects. In the first half of 2020, we have all had to adapt to a new way of living and working, and we have had to embrace greater use of technology, in ways that we may not have anticipated and done so previously, just to stay 'afloat.' These essential adjustments have been for the sake of ourselves, our families, friends and colleagues, as well as communities, and for our financial and economic well-being.

One thing is for sure; the world will never be the same again once we come out of lockdown and once, we resume as 'normal' a life as possible. Amongst other things, one key aspect that we must take forward is the fact that by embracing greater use of technology now, and adapting to new ways of working, which has been a testing ground for us all, this will continue to help us in whatever lies ahead. There will be new threats after Covid-19, and we must learn to adapt to new risks, threats and challenges.

In the family law context, these changes we have made so far, may well enable us to become more efficient in the future, whereby more electronic working will mean less travel, less waiting, potentially less stress, and anxiety for ourselves and indeed, service users. It will inevitably mean that some elements of working in 'lockdown' will survive even when we are out of 'lockdown'.

As an advocate, conducting family litigation, I have found that although there have been added pressures, and difficulties with ensuring technology has worked appropriately for everyone, one thing is for sure, and that is, overall, remote hearings have and can work successfully. It may be that as we venture further out of lockdown, there will be more use of hybrid hearings, so that we may see some hearings, once again taking place face-to-face at court, but some, for purposes of expediency, may continue to be heard remotely. There are obvious advantages to this way of working, and no doubt, court centres will need to adapt and implement such practices across their centres in consultation with service users.

Stay Safe all,

Safda Mahmood

MORE BOOKS BY LAW BRIEF PUBLISHING

A selection of our other titles available now:-

'A Practical Guide to the General Data Protection Regulation (GDPR) – 2nd Edition' by Keith Markham
'Ellis on Credit Hire – Sixth Edition' by Aidan Ellis & Tim Kevan
'A Practical Guide to Working with Litigants in Person and McKenzie Friends in Family Cases' by Stuart Barlow
'Protecting Unregistered Brands: A Practical Guide to the Law of Passing Off' by Lorna Brazell
'A Practical Guide to Secondary Liability and Joint Enterprise Post-Jogee' by Joanne Cecil & James Mehigan
'A Practical Guide to the Pre-Action RTA Claims Protocol for Personal Injury Lawyers' by Antonia Ford
'A Practical Guide to Neighbour Disputes and the Law' by Alexander Walsh
'A Practical Guide to Forfeiture of Leases' by Mark Shelton
'A Practical Guide to Coercive Control for Legal Practitioners and Victims' by Rachel Horman
'A Practical Guide to Rights Over Airspace and Subsoil' by Daniel Gatty
'Tackling Disclosure in the Criminal Courts – A Practitioner's Guide' by Narita Bahra QC & Don Ramble
'A Practical Guide to the Law of Driverless Cars – Second Edition' by Alex Glassbrook, Emma Northey & Scarlett Milligan
'A Practical Guide to TOLATA Claims' by Greg Williams
'Artificial Intelligence – The Practical Legal Issues' by John Buyers
'A Practical Guide to the Law of Prescription in Scotland' by Andrew Foyle
'A Practical Guide to the Construction and Rectification of Wills and Trust Instruments' by Edward Hewitt
'A Practical Guide to the Law of Bullying and Harassment in the Workplace' by Philip Hyland

'How to Be a Freelance Solicitor: A Practical Guide to the SRA-Regulated Freelance Solicitor Model' by Paul Bennett
'A Practical Guide to Prison Injury Claims' by Malcolm Johnson
'A Practical Guide to the Small Claims Track' by Dominic Bright
'A Practical Guide to Advising Clients at the Police Station' by Colin Stephen McKeown-Beaumont
'A Practical Guide to Antisocial Behaviour Injunctions' by Iain Wightwick
'Practical Mediation: A Guide for Mediators, Advocates, Advisers, Lawyers, and Students in Civil, Commercial, Business, Property, Workplace, and Employment Cases' by Jonathan Dingle with John Sephton
'The Mini-Pupillage Workbook' by David Boyle
'A Practical Guide to Crofting Law' by Brian Inkster
'A Practical Guide to Spousal Maintenance' by Liz Cowell
'A Practical Guide to the Law of Domain Names and Cybersquatting' by Andrew Clemson
'A Practical Guide to the Law of Gender Pay Gap Reporting' by Harini Iyengar
'A Practical Guide to the Rights of Grandparents in Children Proceedings' by Stuart Barlow
'NHS Whistleblowing and the Law' by Joseph England
'Employment Law and the Gig Economy' by Nigel Mackay & Annie Powell
'A Practical Guide to Noise Induced Hearing Loss (NIHL) Claims' by Andrew Mckie, Ian Skeate, Gareth McAloon
'An Introduction to Beauty Negligence Claims – A Practical Guide for the Personal Injury Practitioner' by Greg Almond
'Intercompany Agreements for Transfer Pricing Compliance' by Paul Sutton
'Zen and the Art of Mediation' by Martin Plowman
'A Practical Guide to the SRA Principles, Individual and Law Firm Codes of Conduct 2019 – What Every Law Firm Needs to Know' by Paul Bennett
'A Practical Guide to Adoption for Family Lawyers' by Graham Pegg
'A Practical Guide to Industrial Disease Claims' by Andrew Mckie & Ian Skeate
'A Practical Guide to Redundancy' by Philip Hyland
'A Practical Guide to Vicarious Liability' by Mariel Irvine

'A Practical Guide to Applications for Landlord's Consent and Variation of Leases' by Mark Shelton

'A Practical Guide to Relief from Sanctions Post-Mitchell and Denton' by Peter Causton

'A Practical Guide to Equity Release for Advisors' by Paul Sams

'A Practical Guide to Unlawful Eviction and Harassment' by Stephanie Lovegrove

'A Practical Guide to the Law Relating to Food' by Ian Thomas

'A Practical Guide to Financial Services Claims' by Chris Hegarty

'The Law of Houses in Multiple Occupation: A Practical Guide to HMO Proceedings' by Julian Hunt

'A Practical Guide to Unlawful Eviction and Harassment' by Stephanie Lovegrove

'A Practical Guide to Solicitor and Client Costs' by Robin Dunne

'Occupiers, Highways and Defective Premises Claims: A Practical Guide Post-Jackson – 2nd Edition' by Andrew Mckie

'A Practical Guide to Financial Ombudsman Service Claims' by Adam Temple & Robert Scrivenor

'A Practical Guide to the Law of Enfranchisement and Lease Extension' by Paul Sams

'A Practical Guide to Marketing for Lawyers – 2nd Edition' by Catherine Bailey & Jennet Ingram

'A Practical Guide to Advising Schools on Employment Law' by Jonathan Holden

'A Practical Guide to Running Housing Disrepair and Cavity Wall Claims: 2nd Edition' by Andrew Mckie & Ian Skeate

'A Practical Guide to Holiday Sickness Claims – 2nd Edition' by Andrew Mckie & Ian Skeate

'Arguments and Tactics for Personal Injury and Clinical Negligence Claims' by Dorian Williams

'A Practical Guide to QOCS and Fundamental Dishonesty' by James Bentley

'A Practical Guide to Drone Law' by Rufus Ballaster, Andrew Firman, Eleanor Clot

'A Practical Guide to Compliance for Personal Injury Firms Working With Claims Management Companies' by Paul Bennett

'A Practical Guide to the Landlord and Tenant Act 1954: Commercial Tenancies' by Richard Hayes & David Sawtell

'A Practical Guide to Dog Law for Owners and Others' by Andrea Pitt
'RTA Allegations of Fraud in a Post-Jackson Era: The Handbook – 2nd Edition' by Andrew Mckie
'RTA Personal Injury Claims: A Practical Guide Post-Jackson' by Andrew Mckie
'On Experts: CPR35 for Lawyers and Experts' by David Boyle
'An Introduction to Personal Injury Law' by David Boyle
'A Practical Guide to Claims Arising From Accidents Abroad and Travel Claims' by Andrew Mckie & Ian Skeate
'A Practical Guide to Chronic Pain Claims' by Pankaj Madan
'A Practical Guide to Claims Arising from Fatal Accidents' by James Patience
'A Practical Approach to Clinical Negligence Post-Jackson' by Geoffrey Simpson-Scott
'Employers' Liability Claims: A Practical Guide Post-Jackson' by Andrew Mckie
'A Practical Guide to Subtle Brain Injury Claims' by Pankaj Madan
'A Practical Guide to Costs in Personal Injury Cases' by Matthew Hoe
'The No Nonsense Solicitors' Practice: A Guide To Running Your Firm' by Bettina Brueggemann
'The Queen's Counsel Lawyer's Omnibus: 20 Years of Cartoons from The Times 1993-2013' by Alex Steuart Williams

These books and more are available to order online direct from the publisher at www.lawbriefpublishing.com, where you can also read free sample chapters. For any queries, contact us on 0844 587 2383 or mail@lawbriefpublishing.com.

Our books are also usually in stock at www.amazon.co.uk with free next day delivery for Prime members, and at good legal bookshops such as Wildy & Sons.

We are regularly launching new books in our series of practical day-to-day practitioners' guides. Visit our website and join our free newsletter to be kept informed and to receive special offers, free chapters, etc.

You can also follow us on Twitter at www.twitter.com/lawbriefpub.

www.ingramcontent.com/pod-product-compliance
Lightning Source LLC
LaVergne TN
LVHW022117200926
848481LV00003B/1184
9781913715113